GARDEN *Style*

Mary Wynn Ryan

Publications International, Ltd.

Mary Wynn Ryan is the author of *The Ultimate Kitchen, The Ultimate Bath,* and *Cottage Style.* She has written about home furnishings and interior design for various magazines and served as Midwest editor of *Design Times* magazine. Mary also served as director of consumer and trade marketing for the Chicago Merchandise Mart's residential design center. She is president of Winning Ways Marketing, an editorial and marketing consulting firm that specializes in home design and decorating.

Louis Weber, CEO
Publications International, Ltd.
7373 North Cicero Avenue
Lincolnwood, Illinois 60712

Permission is never granted for commercial purposes.

Manufactured in China.

8 7 6 5 4 3 2 1

ISBN: 0-7853-6474-9

Library of Congress Control Number: 2002105955

Contents

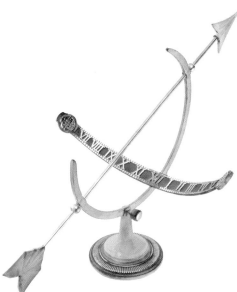

Kitchens & Dining Rooms Alfresco ❀ 34

Fresh air is a natural appetite enhancer, and the experience of dining outdoors always feels a little like a party. Learn how to give your kitchen or dining room delectable garden appeal by using majolica ceramics, floral-pattern dinnerware, and more.

Blooming Living Rooms, Home Offices & Dens ❀ 58

Add a vibrant feeling to living rooms and dens with beautiful garden motifs. Don't forget the home office, where flower power can be equally appealing. After all, what's more conducive to creativity than nature's own masterworks?

Bathroom Oases ❀ 80

Water and gardens go together naturally, so the bath is the perfect place to create your own tropical paradise. A shower of refreshing ideas will help you make a splash with your favorite colors and garden motifs.

Bedroom Bowers ❀ 102

Transform the bedroom into an enchanting retreat. Start with the bed, the room's focal point, and layer on the garden elements. From garden-gate metal beds to picket fence headboards, you'll find a bouquet of ways to fashion a dreamy boudoir.

Resource Directory ❀ 126

The Garden Style State of Mind

I T HAPPENS TO EVERYONE: You're stuck in commuter traffic or chauffeuring the kids, coping with a hectic workday, or just dealing with the stress of the city. Suddenly, you're daydreaming of a place where all you see is cool green and the colors of flowers, all you hear is birdsong, all you feel is warm sunlight on your skin, and all you smell is rain on the lilacs. Welcome to the garden-style state of mind. You're in good company!

Since the beginning of time, the idealized human habitat has been a garden. Combining the beauty of nature and the comforts of civilization, a garden evokes freshness, growth, grace, enchantment, and hope. No wonder garden style appeals to us so deeply.

Of course, it's easiest to live the garden life in a climate that's warm year round, but you can bring that fresh spirit home no matter where you live. All it takes is a crop of garden-inspired furnishings and decorating strategies like the ones you'll find in this book. You don't even need a house with land to garden. Some of the most endearing garden rooms are magically evoked in high-rise apartments.

While real gardens can be a tough row to hoe, garden style is easy to cultivate. So many home furnishings, accessories, and artwork carry garden-related motifs that the only challenge is in picking the look you like best. Whether your taste is formal or casual, traditional or modern, all-American or cosmopolitan, you can find a way to express the nurturing, lively spirit of garden style.

Cultivate Your Garden Spirit

Take a leisurely walk through these pages, and you'll see a world of garden inspirations for every room of the house. You'll discover breezy porches and sunrooms, kitchens and dining rooms alfresco, living rooms in bloom, flower-powered home offices, bathroom oases, and bedrooms that are irrepressibly romantic floral bowers. And if you see a dining room scheme

Romantic and relaxed, this nostalgic porch area evokes English garden style with a tropical, British Colonial twist. Rattan easy chairs, pretty pillows, and an exotic screen mixed with antique treasures and fresh blooms make an inviting scene.

Like a cozy Victorian bed-and-breakfast, this room is filled with pampering touches and garden inspirations. A colorful, traditional floral takes center stage, its bright hues balanced by lots of white and blue. When you find a garden print you love, use it lavishly. Interior designer: Ann Platz.

chic. Chartreuse is edgy and witty, and, because it contains so much yellow, it evokes the warmth of sunshine, too. When it comes to garden style, it's hard to go wrong with green.

Of course, just as flowers come in every hue, so does garden style, which gives you a lot of latitude. For example, say you have a passion for poppy, sunflower, and iris blue, or you enjoy a casual lifestyle and great food, or you're in love with Impressionist paintings. Why not take decorating inspiration from the French countryside and the gardens of Monet? If you like flower pastels and rich antique woods, lots of books, and fabrics that can stand up to a dog or two, why not let romantic English country style set your garden scheme?

What if your personal style is more spare and modern? A crisp, cool background of green and white lattice delivers garden flair in a chic, contemporary way. Lattice or trellis designs can be especially appealing if you're working with a small apartment home or any small room where you want an airy, spacious feeling. For another take on the clean, minimalist approach, consider Asian garden style. It's possibly the world's most eloquent way of expressing reverence for nature and simplicity. Just add a bit of lacquer black or cinnabar (red-orange) to your green and white scheme, and use white spider mums or orchids as your flowers.

On the other hand, garden style can be just plain fun, so if you get a kick out of that retro-Polynesian look of the 1940s and 1950s, indulge! Find yourself some kitschy hibiscus prints and some vintage metal porch furniture for a fun, hip look.

You don't have to make green a major player to create a garden scheme, as long as this color is in there somewhere. If your favorite color combination is blue, yellow, and white, treat yourself to that sunny scheme: A palette that might otherwise say "beach" can as easily say "garden" if you pick a bunch of pretty floral blue, yellow, and white prints with green leaves. Whatever you like best, mix up elements to please yourself. Garden style offers a lot of room for free-spirited expression.

As you browse this book, take note of captivating details, too. Birdhouses, baskets, garden tools, watering cans, rose trellises, botanical watercolors, and garden statuary are among the many accents that can bring your scheme to life. If, like many people, you already collect decorative frogs, birds, lady-

you love, feel free to import it to a bedroom or living room. Garden style is relaxed, romantic, and even a bit whimsical, so the look flows easily from one room to another.

Pick Your Garden Palette

As you leaf through this book, take note of color schemes and decorating themes that speak to you personally. Just about any scheme that includes liberal amounts of green and white evokes garden style. You'll often see green, white, and deep pink put to work beautifully in this way, even in living rooms. Another proven crowd-pleaser is green, white, and red—including coral, scarlet, crimson, or burgundy. The timeless complementary colors red and green can represent any personality: Think regal Victorian roses, lush tropical ferns and hibiscus, or cheery geraniums.

If you don't already have a favorite shade of green, remember that deep hunter green is classically elegant, mid-tone kelly green is always popular, and lime green is youthful and bugs, or other garden creatures, group three or more for impact or let one peek out from behind a plant here and there. Use a footed birdbath as a low occasional table for your keys and mail. Whimsical touches like these are perfect for lighthearted garden style.

While most garden-style rooms are a casual mix of motifs, you can home in on specific natural motifs that fit especially well with certain established styles. For example, Arts & Crafts style is associated with stylized lotus blossoms, oaks, acorns, and the occasional frisky squirrel. French Country favors sunflowers and poppies, and English Country means roses, ivy, rabbits, and field mice (think Beatrix Potter). American Country is mad for ducks and daisies, while vintage style is sweet on bluebirds, violets, and geraniums. Tropical style features ferns, orchids, hibiscus, tiny lizards, exotic butterflies, and graceful herons or cranes. You get the idea. If your taste runs to one of these established looks, it should be fairly

easy to find wallcoverings and fabrics to anchor your scheme. Then you can fill in with finds of your own.

Even if collecting isn't your thing, you can use everyday household items to create a garden feeling in any room. You'll want bowls and platters, candlesticks, table linens, bed linens, paper napkins, toss pillows, and more. So shop for designs that further your fresh garden look. Charming natural motifs have come to a wider-than-ever range of products, including drapery rod finials shaped like elm leaves or acorns. You can find kitchen or bath cabinet hardware shaped like oak leaves, frogs, and flowers, so it's easy to bring a fanciful garden feeling to these utilitarian spaces. Whatever room you're decorating, even a few key elements in the garden motif can carry the message.

If you're up for a bigger project, you can give your room a fresh, inviting atmosphere with garden-inspired backgrounds. One way is to use a trio of color-coordinated large-, medium-, and small-scale floral prints for wallcoverings, upholstered furniture, and window treatments. If that's a bit too much of a good thing for you, pick one wonderful floral fabric plus a coordinating geometric print and a solid color. And remember, you don't have to pick true florals: There are beautiful patterns of ferns and other greenery that create the same fresh feeling with a slightly more tailored effect. For kitchens and dining rooms, consider fabrics depicting luscious fruits or vegetables. They're available in many styles, from opulent Renaissance to funky '50s.

Regardless of what decorating scheme you adopt, capture all the bright warmth of sunshine you can with breezy or minimal window treatments. If you need heavier ones for privacy, floral draperies are a natural, but be sure you can draw them wide to let the sun shine in. If you prefer plain draperies, you can also give them a lighthearted, garden feeling if you use good-quality silk vines, flowering or not, as tiebacks. Consider

Dragonflies on white cushions and leafy vines on soft yellow pillows produce a cool, sophisticated garden scheme that's contemporary. Black metal furniture, as spare as can be, makes a crisp contrast to ornate architectural fragments. Manufacturer: Stroheim & Romann.

Glass-top tables used bare are practical outdoors, but on a sheltered porch try a tablecloth topper. This casual, low-key look gets a shot of drama from the curvy iron furniture and the even more eye-catching topiary plants. Manufacturer: Seabrook Wallcoverings.

conventional metal tiebacks shaped like leaves and blossoms as another option. Bamboo shades lend an exotic, tropical feeling, and white-painted shutters provide cottage charm. Pleated shades look clean and graceful; best are the models that draw down from the top of the window, affording privacy while offering a view.

When it comes to flooring, choose natural or outdoor-type materials. Wood is a natural, but patio brick, slate pavers, and rustic tiles are especially exciting ways to create a terrace effect underfoot. For maximum outdoors impact, you can extend the same flooring from a semi-enclosed porch or sun-room into an interior room, and warm things up with a floral, needlepoint area rug. Small scatter rugs that look like giant, realistic pansies or roses are widely available and make a fun statement in even the tiniest room.

You'll find more wallcoverings with floral motifs than just about any other kind, but don't overlook those with vines, ferns, and other images of nonflowering greenery nor those with stylized trellis and lattice motifs. If you prefer a hand-painted finish, the classic technique of trompe l'oeil—painting that fools the eye—is wonderfully romantic and can transform any room in the house.

This sleekly handsome room, open to an adjoining patio garden, combines Eastern simplicity and eclectic wit. Garden sculpture brought indoors, cool tile and sisal flooring, and a few superb live plants create a confident look that's up-to-the-minute. Interior designer: Accent On Design.

Neoclassical elegance comes to life in a coolly graceful dining room. A masterful trompe l'oeil painting of a Renaissance palace garden creates subtle depth and drama. The sophisticated scheme of bisque, stone, terra-cotta, and black proves how rich neutral colors can be. Interior designer: Cross Interiors.

Trompe l'oeil lends itself to grand gestures. Imagine how that cramped little hallway would look when transformed with an arched trellis overlooking a vista of gardens, fields, and orchards. Or how that flat dining room would look with a neoclassical wall niche containing a gorgeous vase of flowers. Even a simple flowering vine, hand painted around the head of a bed or around a bathroom mirror, creates a lighthearted garden feeling. For the look of a fairy-tale castle, have flowering vines growing from between faux-limestone bricks in a little powder room. Or, for a lavish, utterly romantic garden look, have antique columns wrapped in tendrils of vines reaching up into a blue, cloud-strewn sky on your ceiling.

Trompe l'oeil inspirations abound in art books about ancient Greece and Rome, Renaissance Italy, and England of the Romantic period (early 1800s), and the technique is extremely popular today. If you can't find a trompe l'oeil artist under "decorative painters" in the phone book or at your

local art school, consider stencils. Advertised in the classified sections of home decorating and do-it-yourself magazines, multilayered stencils let you create large-scale, sophisticated garden murals anywhere in your home.

Enlist the sense of smell when weaving your garden spell. When you can't open all the windows to let fresh air in, bring in the light scents of flowers, fruits, herbs, and greenery with scented candles and potpourri. But do keep it light, and shop until you find high-quality, naturalistic scents. This is one place where spending a bit more can make a real difference. Cool eucalyptus and pungent lavender are available as naturally scented dried flowers; some fresh flowers, such as freesia, hyacinth, and stargazer lilies, also have strong, sweet scents that can last a week or more. For a short-term infusion of uplifting scent, simply peel an orange. To waft scents subtly around your room or to provide comfortable air circulation, install a simple wood ceiling fan. It's an easy way to evoke a relaxing, tropical feeling.

Decorating With Cut Flowers and Potted Plants

Obviously, the easiest way to create a springtime garden home is to grow your own cut flowers, but that's not always practical. You don't have to be rich, however, to buy cut flowers on a weekly basis for your home, because even supermarkets carry flowers these days. Skip the usually color-clashing, premade bouquets and look for mini carnations, baby's breath, statice, chrysanthemums, and Asian lilies that you can combine to create your own casual bouquets. They come in a nice range of colors and blooms that last for a week or more if you change the water daily. (Keep cut flowers out of direct sunlight to preserve them longer.)

If you do succumb to a bouquet that includes irises or other quick-fading beauties, be sure to pull out the dead blooms each day, tweak your arrangement to rebalance the remaining blossoms, and replace the water. Talk to a flower lover for a few simple tips on keeping your cut flowers going. For example, a few drops of chlorine bleach will keep water fresh longer, and a penny in the vase will prevent tulips from opening too fast.

If your place receives a reasonable amount of sun, shop for flowering potted plants such as cyclamen, geraniums, lilies, or,

if you can afford it, orchids. Then learn how to keep them happy. If green plants suit you best, look for ivy, asparagus ferns, philodendrons, or shade-tolerant peace lilies. Whatever the live plants in your garden-style scheme may be, make sure they're good specimens in superb health.

Cheerful yellow chairs with yellow linen cushions seem to capture the sunlight from the windows above. A chic floral wallcovering in gold, green, and brown on yellow gives the sitting area a spunky, light-hearted feeling. Manufacturer: Maine Cottage.

Learn what kinds of conditions the plants you favor require. Old metal or porcelain trays are great for keeping damp pots off furniture. Whatever you do, resist the temptation to treat live plants as strictly decorative accessories. Most need healthy amounts of sun to give their best display, especially the flowering varieties, so don't try to use a live plant to brighten a dark corner. Instead use vases of cut flowers or good-quality, realistic-looking silk flowers and plants.

Whether your plants are real, faux, or a mix of each, show them off in woven baskets, porcelain cachepots, and pottery planters that make great decorating statements by themselves. Don't overlook less traditional planters, though. If you received an extra silver-plated ice bucket as a wedding gift, use it to hold that prized orchid plant and use that old copper cooking pot as a charming home for a cascading English ivy.

Stroll through the pages of *Garden Style: Bringing the Outdoors In* and gather a bouquet of decorating inspirations to create your own personal Eden. Relaxing, refreshing, and always hopeful, garden style makes coming home a beautiful experience in any season.

Breezy Porches & Sunrooms

INDOOR-OUTDOOR ROOMS take naturally to garden style. Any space with a defined floor and overhead protection can extend your living area out-of-doors. All it takes is a patio with an awning or arbor. If you're decorating an open porch or a screened porch exposed to the elements, opt for easy-care, weather-resistant furnishings and keep accessories simple. If your space is a sunroom or other enclosed room with lots of glass, you can use conventional furniture and protect it from sun damage by using window coatings or simple shades. For a fun, fresh look, choose real porch furniture. Airy wicker and rattan are appealing classics that come in practical all-weather versions. Wrought iron is a pretty tradition; aluminum is lightweight, rustproof, and available in sleek contemporary as well as traditional styles. For romantic end tables, try stone or faux-stone columns. For accessories, use wonderful architectural fragments, antique gardening tools, and old pots. Bring your favorite flower prints and colors into the setting with upholstery and soft accessories. Today's fabrics for outdoor-furniture cushions look close to indoor upholstery, plus they're mildew-resistant. Finally, load a garden bench or fill a tea cart with your favorite potted plants—indoors or out, they make the look.

An entryway sets the garden tone with a woven wicker chair and an architectural pedestal displaying a vase of cut flowers. The faux vines and leaves hand-painted on the wall enhance the casually romantic look.

To wake up your sunroom's palette, choose a vibrant flower color. In this airy yet dramatic setting, wicker furniture displays a coat of deep ruby red instead of the expected white or hunter green. An opulent rose print ties in the deep red with the room's predominantly white tints, so the look is lively but not jarring. Manufacturer: Renaissance Conservatories.

Languid Afternoons

WICKER, RATTAN, CANE, reeds, and rushes have been woven into furniture since earliest times. Sturdy and lightweight, woven furniture copes relatively well with moisture, so it has always been at home in humid and tropical climes. Today, you can buy all-weather wicker and rattan made of woven synthetic fiber or natural fiber with a waterproof coating. They can brave most weather, although they can't be repainted. Whatever the material, the look is relaxing. Painted white or a pastel tint, woven furniture looks lighthearted; finished in a natural hue or a dark, rich color, it looks downright exotic. You can further the look with decorative accessories, planters, and fabrics of choice for furniture cushions. In the sunrooms, rose-print fabrics in retro colors and in gentle, muted tones set a nostalgic mood. Sisal floor covering underscores the versatile appeal of natural woven fibers.

Opposite: This sunroom-porch affords a sense of casual graciousness. Floor-to-ceiling sliding doors get an elegant, traditional look with divided lite windowpanes. Cushions and pillows in soft tones enhance the feeling of bygone days.

Right: Garden style can be brilliant. With the graceful curve of an arbor in the background, this lipstick-red wicker chair and its polka-dot cushions create a surprising, witty pattern play to wake up a shady garden area. Furniture can be painted to echo flower colors. Manufacturer: Maine Cottage.

Left: Brick pavers laid in a herringbone pattern, comfortable wicker barrel chairs, and lots of flourishing plants establish an inviting garden mood on this sunny, enclosed porch. A washable quilt makes a casual, colorful tablecloth with the appeal of an impromptu picnic. Interior designer: Carol Fink. Architect/ Manufacturer: Alpine Log Homes.

Brightly Inviting

WHETHER YOUR SETTING is a shady outdoor spot or a sunny indoor place, bring your garden decorating scheme to life with a punch of color. Green is a natural hue that's both warm and cool, and it looks great with just about any other color. That goes for the neutral, natural tones of weathered brick and wood, too. Both of these spaces use brilliant red and white to create a lively accent. Turquoise, coral, hot pink, periwinkle (blue-violet), or chartreuse (yellow with a touch of lime) would look wonderful also. Timeless wicker and rattan furniture goes a long way toward creating a breezy, relaxed feeling and looks great in a natural or colored finish.

*Favorite old-fashioned peren-
nials and annuals mix it up
in colorful fashion along the
base of the faux-stone walls in
this room. The charming
treatment can make even a
tiny foyer look more open.
Enhance the look by repeating
flower colors in a brightly
painted garden bench and
accessories. Manufacturer:
Seabrook Wallcoverings.*

Forecast: Sunny and Bright

SUFFUSED WITH SUNLIGHT streaming through a real window and a lattice-covered loggia, these charming spaces share the blithe spirit of summer. Wallcoverings that mimic masterful trompe l'oeil painted scenes are key to these lighthearted looks. Against faux-stone walls, flowers grow and cottage windows open to the air. You apply these giant trompe l'oeil scenes as you would any matched-pattern wallcovering. As with a theatrical backdrop, once this is in place, it takes only a few key furnishings to complete the fantasy environment. If you want to include specific personal items in your trompe l'oeil setting, you need to find a specialty painter, but if you don't, your choice of wallcoverings is broad enough to satisfy just about any dream scheme. Stone walls, chinked log walls, latticework, and more are available, already embellished with beguiling little accents. They look great anywhere, especially in a small foyer.

White-painted trelliswork lets in dappled sunlight or makes a lacy false ceiling to conceal lighting fixtures overhead. Windows framed in blue shutters and an array of cheerful red geraniums, real and faux, create a fun French country mood. *Manufacturer: Seabrook Wallcoverings.*

Playful Romantics

A REAL GARDEN STRETCHING out as far as the eye can see: the perfect view. Look to faux finishing and trompe l'oeil painting techniques to bring an air of refreshing elegance to an ordinary space. These two dining spots, one on a veranda and one a grand illusion, share a spirited kinship. In one, European opulence takes on a whimsical, tongue-in-chic mood, thanks to silk vines that frame windows and faux-stone walls open to summer skies. In the other, the porch's ruglike floor border and interior-style draperies agreeably blur the distinction between indoors and out. With backgrounds like these, airy furniture of any kind—wicker, rattan, metal, and glass—and lots of fresh, flowering plants are all you need.

Right: Sometimes you want to pull out all the stops for romance. Airy wire peacock chairs and a glass-top table give a lighthearted effect that lets the garden accents stand out. Faux-stone walls, a blue-sky-and-pansy border, vine-draped cottage windows, and topiaries create a fairy-tale mood. Manufacturer: Seabrook Wallcoverings.

Left: A spectacular rotunda porch attains an extraordinary sense of romance with just a few homey touches. A wood floor with a leafy border takes on the aspect of an area rug, and the full, gathered draperies give open areas a comfortable, semi-enclosed feeling. A palette restricted to hunter green and white adds to the timeless grace.

This sunroom is livable any time of year, thanks to radiators hidden under the black granite windowsill. With enough light to support large plants and even specimen trees, this room enjoys the balmy feeling of a conservatory. Old-fashioned wrought-iron and wicker furniture carries out the sentimental scheme.

Sentimental Journey

ONSERVATORY SUNROOMS AND wide veranda porches are hallmarks of 19th-century style at its most romantic. So if you love old white lace and flower colors, these settings are the perfect places to indulge them. Whether your space is old or new, a fresh coat of white paint will lend a soothing air to everything it touches. Set off against clean white, a complementary color scheme of pink and green has been a foolproof favorite since Victorian times. For an updated, equally beguiling effect, try lilac or coral plus green. Healthy plants, large and small, are major players in these settings because there's plenty of sunlight to go around. Just as important are beautiful old table linens and frankly flowered pillows. Layer them as you please for a sweetly individual look.

Old, ornate wire porch furniture is as romantic as can be, and the addition of plump floral pillows makes it comfortable, too. The pretty tea cart is practical for impromptu entertaining any time. An airy pergola overhead lets in enough sun for thriving ivy topiaries, lupines, and even roses.

Natural Charms

I F YOU'RE NATURALLY INCLINED toward garden style, then chances are you've already collected an array of accessories to bring the look home. Extra-casual living spaces, such as the porch and potting shed shown here, are easy to decorate with rustic basics. But any casual space, from family room to sunroom, can benefit from the same treatment. A relaxing mix of vintage wood, wicker, and twig pieces works perfectly well together. Washable cotton chintz or cotton duck covers are inviting to kids, dogs, and all manner of casual guests. Simple, naturalistic accessories look nice here, so consider grouping collections that have similar themes. If you collect birdhouses or birdcages and your spouse collects carved wooden birds, stage them together for a witty statement. Ditto if you collect pressed flowers and he likes antique gardening tools. Group a few of each for a look that's charming, naturally.

Above: *An old potting shed gets a sunny, fresh outlook thanks to bright yellow and white paint. Potting tables and plant stands offer plenty of ways to care for plants.* Interior designer: The Comfort Common. Above left: *A rose trellis doesn't have to be garden size to make a charming, outdoorsy impression. A scaled-down version shows off blooms and has architectural interest, too. Use real roses in direct sun and high-quality silk ones like these elsewhere.* Manufacturer: NDI.

Right: *A medley of antique garden implements, birdhouses, and vintage furniture makes a soothing retreat of a simple, open porch. A few artful accents, including a button-covered lampshade and a floral painting, establish an appealing personality that lifts the look beyond mere comfort.*

Black and White in Color

WE OFTEN THINK of black, white, and gray as chic and chilly, best suited to a minimalist, modern setting. But these austere tones can also have a place in garden-inspired schemes. Black and white make a splendid sophisticated foil to any flower color, from pale pink to flaming red. In fact, in a predominantly black-and-white setting, it takes only a few colorful flowers to create visual excitement. The outdoor living areas here illustrate the point with panache. The owners have chosen black metal or white wood and wicker furniture and confined all the color to plants and flowers. Black-and-white checkerboard flooring, a formal choice since classical times, looks fresh and sassy on a rooftop garden and a porch. Try the crisp geometry of black and white and see how it brightens your greenery and flower colors.

Opposite: High atop a city apartment building, astilbe and foxgloves in pink and white add soft sparks of color to the urban setting. Potted topiary plants hang on the chimney, further softening the scene. Black and white stones laid in a checkerboard pattern define the space with graphic drama. Interior designer: Madison Cox.

Right: Marbled tile flooring in a black-and-white checkerboard pattern wakes up this sleepily romantic porch with unexpected punch. Wood and wicker furniture pieces are united by a distressed white finish. Against this cool background, a spray of red and purple blooms makes an exciting statement.

Full-height windows overlook a handsome garden, but the indoor view is lovely, too. A fabulous floral upholstery fabric sets a warm, sophisticated color scheme, and cane furniture enhances the slightly exotic, elegant feeling. A few large-scale tropical plants plus cut flowers in the room's color scheme add just the right finishing touches.
Interior designer: Justine Ringlien.

This sunroom imparts an air of drama and fantasy with its wonderful array of decoratively painted, scrolled, and upholstered furniture and the stunning effect of the painted leafy branches that reach across the ceiling. Manufacturer: Renaissance Conservatories.

Eloquent Statements

ROMANTIC STYLE, A CONCEPT begun in the 1800s, celebrates the wildness of nature as being inherently beautiful without giving up creature comforts. This perspective is alive and well in opulent, garden-inspired rooms. So bring on that luxurious, colorful, whimsical style that makes a garden room so appealing. How to start? If you have a glorious floral rug, use it as a focal point and echo the tones in more subdued upholstery patterns. If you love an exuberant floral upholstery pattern, let it be the star. Fill in with accent furniture in faux bois (woodgraining) or trompe l'oeil-decorated wood, plus curvy pieces in wicker, cane, tortoiseshell bamboo, and other exotic woods. Tall floor plants are a must. If you like trompe l'oeil foliage on the walls, carry your garden inspiration to new heights and extend it up onto the ceiling. Keep the windows uncovered to bring the garden view indoors.

Neoclassical Perspective

WHETHER YOUR ENTRY area is vast or tiny, trompe l'oeil can create a great sense of dimension as well as visual interest. Find inspiration for trompe l'oeil scenes in art books: Paintings from the Renaissance through the Romantic eras yield wonderful vistas of castles, cottages, and country-sides. Antique architectural drawings of neoclassical buildings also offer heart-lifting inspiration. A tal-ented specialty painter should be able to approximate the look for you; if you can't find a professional in your area, ask at local commu-nity colleges and art fairs. If you lack the room or the floor depth to view a full-size scene, consider painting an elegant little win-dow niche overlooking a small-scale view of neigh-boring hills and gardens. The scene can be painted directly onto a wall or onto a prepared board that you can take with you if you move.

Left: *Elegant antique instruments and garden statuary create a timeless feeling in this foyer, but the formal mood is balanced by a trio of giant conch shells casually strewn on an old wicker table. Near the window are light-loving plants; the urn away from the window holds a shade-tolerant peace lily.* Above: *A footed urn elevates distinctive flowering plants to new heights of elegance. Coordinating vase and blossom colors is a foolproof way to create visual unity. If you don't like to see stems, an opaque vase like this is best; just be sure to change the water daily for live flowers.* Manufacturer: NDI.

A tiny nook attains magical proportions with an enchanting mix of trompe l'oeil paintings, a neoclassical urn, and beautiful tropical plants. Orchids and other exotics like these need lots of light, ample humidity, and protection from cold drafts, but their lovely blooms last a long time.

Exotic Interlude

HESE FOYERS DO more than welcome guests: They transport visitors into a beguiling world. Masterful use of color is key. A fearless artistry in these glowing tones invites you in, just as an entry hall is supposed to do. Once inside, you're drawn to the unique touches that make these rooms a reflection of their owners. Trompe l'oeil transforms one space into a grape arbor that seems taken from old Italy; a dramatic mirror and heavily carved demi-lune (half-moon) table give the other space a sense of drama that recalls Moorish Spain. With imaginative wall treatments, nicely detailed furniture, and a few carefully chosen accessories, even a tiny front hall can set the stage for the drama of your life. So pull out the stops, put out the items that make you smile, and have fun with it.

Opposite: Glorious melding tones of gold and turquoise combine to create a range of soothing, almost hypnotic aquarium greens on the walls and window frames of this unique foyer. A meandering pattern of grapevines and fruit enhances the flowing, surreal atmosphere.

Left: A spectacular antique mirror and demi-lune table make a dramatic first impression, but the look lightens up with an array of novel accessories. Walls in a golden wash are a lovely complement to deep green accents. Interior designer: Madison Cox.

Timeless Elegance

Frrom the smallest foyer with its single chair to the most spacious sunroom with two or three seating groups, any garden room deserves great furnishings. Fortunately, manufacturers have responded to the current desire for upscale outdoor living with designs as elegant as any for indoors. Now it's easier than ever to blur the boundaries between indoors and out. To begin, establish your home's garden theme right away at the front door with a distinctive little bench, eye-catching planters, or a pretty chair. Continue the airy look with more pieces from the same collection in adjoining rooms. If you like the spare look of slatted wood or metal (certainly easy to care for!) but want more comfort for everyday use, take your pick of cushions in great-looking outdoor fabrics. Pair contemporary prints with contemporary furniture, or create eclectic appeal with today's prints on nostalgic frames. Welcome home!

Outdoor furniture can be of investment quality. This traditional American estate furniture, constructed of mahogany or teak, is made with marine carpentry techniques and finishing. It will stand up beautifully on a porch or in a sunroom. Source: Brennan-Edwards.

Garden ornaments should be few and chosen for their distinctive charm, as is clear in this sculpture-cum-plant stand. Cast in stone from an artifact found in an English garden, it holds a 5-inch pot. Source: Smith & Hawken.

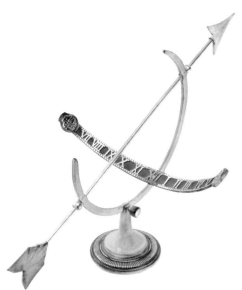

Marking only the happy hours, sundials rank among the most intriguing of garden ornaments. Inspired by classical antiquities, this armillary sundial is crafted of solid brass with verdigris highlights. Source: Krupps.com.

Hang this handsome window grate planter inside or out to hold 8-inch pots. Re-created from an iron grille found at an English manor, the planter is 42 inches high, 36 inches wide, and comes in dark verde or burnished copper. Source: Ballard Designs.

The soothing sound of trickling water is enhanced by the pleasing, round shapes and placid, aqua-blue glaze of this handthrown pottery fountain. Measuring 13×9 inches, this three-tier fountain of tranquility fits anywhere. Source: Coldwater Creek.

The dramatic, yet whimsically Dr. Seuss-like look of a pony-tail palm makes it perfect for a tropical room that doesn't take itself too seriously. One palm is a great accent; two or more is an oasis. A woven basket completes the look. Manufacturer: Natural Decorations, Inc. (NDI).

You don't have to be the flowery type to enjoy garden style and create it in your home. Bring your room to verdant life with botanically inspired accent pillows that depict a variety of graceful green ferns. Manufacturer: Michaelian & Kohlberg.

Chinese-style jardinières (garden stools), like this one with vibrantly hand-painted tobacco leaf motifs, have been classic garden accents for ages. Often used as an end table to lighten a formal room, the porcelain seat adds a refined touch. Source: Gump's.

Recalling the airy charm and chic confidence of French bistro style, this Parisian armchair is crafted of wrought iron in a soft, subtle shade of green that blends into any garden environment. Manufacturer: Summer Classics.

Kitchens & Dining Rooms Alfresco

ARMFULS OF FLOWERS and baskets of fresh-picked fruits bring homegrown charm to your kitchen and give your dining room an air of natural hospitality. But you don't need a green thumb to create a garden-inspired decorating scheme. From wallcoverings and borders to chair cushions and pot holders, decorating products with garden motifs abound. These days, products designed for the kitchen can be sophisticated. That's not too surprising, because the ideal kitchen is big, beautiful, and open to spaces that are often elegantly decorated. It's easier than ever to create a lovely look that flows from room to room. To cook up an overall theme, choose elegant Renaissance urns filled with fruits and flowers, charming baskets of English ivy, or whatever garden motif appeals to you. Blend in a compatible color scheme, perhaps a vintage wine, olive, and gold or a crisp white and green. If your look is American country, use stencils to extend your motifs; if you prefer the ambience of a European manor, consider trompe l'oeil paintings of garden vistas. Whatever your taste, garden style is an appetizing option.

Opposite: On a balcony a dining table is set up invitingly with tablecloths, chair covers, and dinnerware of pink, a flower color that complements the elegant tableware as well as the myriad shades of green in the potted plants and trees. **Above:** *For a kitchen decorating touch that's whimsical yet chic, consider these large-scale pears, 9½ or 11½ inches high. Made of hand-glazed terra-cotta, they're accented with a bronzy leaf and stem. Use one as a casual tabletop accent or a pair as bookends for your prized cookbooks.* Source: *Ballard Designs.*

Romantic Recollections

TRADITIONALLY STYLED PURE white cabinets with dark gray or black stone counters are elegant. But what about bringing warmth, ease, and a bit of romance to such a handsome kitchen? Trust rich, red roses, stargazer lilies, and the like to bring all this to the table. Add the surprise of real upholstered furniture, and the stage is set for casual dining that's downright pampering. Choose a dark-tone, multicolor needlepoint that hides spills or some washable, cotton-blend slipcovers for an easy-care yet elegant look. Build up the indulgent garden look with floral window treatments, place mats, and other accent fabrics, as well as decorative accessories displaying your favorite fruits and flowers. In a setting this appealing, a simple bouquet of choice blooms or a small flowering plant in a cachepot makes a perfect little centerpiece.

Tall, imposing arrangements are fine on a sideboard or an entry hall table if the room is spacious, but for a dining table you want something different. A low, lacy arrangement that lets diners see each other across the table is essential. Draping vines can extend the scale without hiding guests. Manufacturer: NDI.

Above: Cupboards at least 12 inches below the ceiling offer ample room to display a collection of garden-inspired accessories. Use silk plants atop cupboards because live ones need more light and less heat. Flowered needlepoint chair seats add a romantic French touch. Interior designer: Durene Phillipo Designs. *Left: Slipper chairs, all dolled up in a pretty, old-fashioned print of cabbage roses, pair with a tablecloth of lacy cutwork to give this practical kitchen an unexpectedly romantic feeling. To make this look hassle-free, choose washable, loose-fitting cotton chintz slipcovers and a cotton or cotton-blend tablecloth.*

Sky-blue paint visually widens this area and sets the stage for an enchanting breakfast room that opens to a magic garden. If you have a small, nondescript room or hall, the illusion of the outdoors on the whole surface of an end wall can be captivating.

A parade of colorful faux flower baskets gives guests a delightful reason to look up in this playful kitchen. Even more appealing, rustic bird-houses and spring flowers transform the island with homegrown charm. Freehand artistry, elaborate stencils, and, in some cases, extra-wide wallpaper borders can achieve similar effects. Manufacturer: Seabrook Wallcoverings.

Happy With the Blues

BLUE SKIES: WHO EVER gets enough of them? These owners decided to bring fair weather indoors, with delightfully creative results. Most blues, like most greens, look soothing with just about any other hue, so you can create a garden of paintbox colors. Blue backgrounds offer another decorating plus, because blue is a cool, recessive hue that makes any room look a bit more spacious. Trompe l'oeil garden scenes, big or small, seem at their best against blue the color of the sky.

Gloriously carved crown moldings would be romantic enough for most people, but these owners went a step further, opening a hole in the ceiling to let in a faux view of trees and birds against a cloud-strewn sky. Live cooking herbs in pots thrive in the sunny sink window. Interior designer: Barton Lidsky, The Hammer & Nail.

European Flavor

A big fruit bowl ornaments the commercial range's backsplash; grape clusters parade across the range hood and are echoed in the vine trim on the cabinets and the hanging lamp. It all adds up to a lavish Italianate look. Interior designer: D'Image/Fran Murphy & Associates.

F YOU LIKE A SUN-WARMED, outdoorsy feeling but don't want to give up on gloriously civilized design and architectural elements, indulge in Country French or Italian style. Enormously popular, especially in areas where warm weather lingers, these looks celebrate opulent design and rich flavors. Italian and French country gardens are filled with luscious ripened fruits, including grapes, tomatoes, and olives, as well as sturdy, drought-resistant sunflowers, poppies, and lavender. Italian and French gardens are also home to wonderful cooking herbs. Put these earthy delights together with cabinets and trims elaborately carved with grapevines and other natural motifs, and you have the recipe for a classic. To complete the look, pick Italian tiles painted with colorful garden motifs and wrought-iron accents, such as bar chairs and pendant lamps, with fruit, leaf, and vine designs. The layering of details adds up to a rich cornucopia of garden charms.

Showcasing Collections

KITCHENS AND DINING ROOMS are great places to display accessories and collections inspired by cooking and gardening hobbies. You may have amassed such a grouping without noticing it. Ceramic or porcelain dishes, copper molds, cookpots, cookie cutters, enameled tin trays, brass candlesticks, gardening tools, salt-and-pepper shakers, and many other items with a garden motif can end up in your collection. You could stash them out of sight if your decorating scheme is formal. But if you enjoy relaxed, romantic garden style, why not leave your treasures out? Just group them for visual impact. If you can hang them, paint the wall behind them a flattering hue: Copper looks great against blue-green, and silver or pewter is lovely against periwinkle blue-violet. If you can display them in a cabinet, use one that complements the feeling of the collection.

Whimsical yet rich, a gorgeous collection of vintage English ceramics deserves the royal treatment. Even if your collection is not of museum quality, it is worth a display that lets you enjoy it every day. Gather your favorites in a handsome piece of furniture and/or hang them on a wall.

A wonderful, old, pine Welsh sideboard is a grand showcase for a world-class collection of vintage floral ceramics. Curtains in a jonquil-yellow floral print take their color cue from the predominantly yellow and pink pieces; the curtain ruffle echoes the charming scalloped face frame of the sideboard.

Fresh-Picked and Fearless

CABINETS AND APPLIANCES fill a fair amount of space in the average kitchen, but you can enlist walls, ceilings, and even cabinet fronts to carry out your garden theme. The effect can be delightfully theatrical or soothingly subtle, as shown in these two kitchens. If you want to go all-out, look for coordinating wallcovering and border collections that depict the flowers, fruits, or vegetables you like. For a more quiet effect, have a trompe l'oeil scene painted, perhaps with a calligraphic message, and use more conventional kitchen elements to continue the scheme. Whether your taste tends toward orchard brights or antique floral hues, use a variety of greens for a foolproof garden feeling. Majolica plates and all kinds of kitchenware patterned after garden elements are naturals for extra decoration, so put them out where friends and family can enjoy them.

Practical kitchen accessories don't have to look utilitarian. Faintly tinted fruits and flowers against a brick-red background make this simple battery clock a pretty choice for any traditional kitchen. Made of wood with an aged look, it measures 14 inches. Source: Ballard Designs.

"The wilderness shall blossom as the rose." This biblical quote festoons the wall treatment above the window, setting the tone for a happy mix of retro cooking tools, country accents, and decorative tiles in a range of greens. A bump-out garden window gives the windowsill herbs a sunny outlook.

This fun kitchen evokes the sweet appeal of an old-time apple orchard. Wallcovering coordinates are key: Large-scale borders give the effect of still-life paintings; small-scale borders with laser-cut edges have a 3-D look; and the tablecloth-check lends a picnic air. The "lettuce" majolica adds a finishing garden touch. *Manufacturer: Seabrook Wallcovering.*

Fabulous ferns star in this sunny breakfast room. A casual dining group is scaled for comfort but doesn't visually overwhelm the space, thanks to its airy design, white color, and clear glass tabletop. Chairs on casters make impromptu entertaining easy.

Sunshine State

A KITCHEN IS THE PERFECT place to express your sunny, colorful outlook on garden style. This kitchen takes the soft blue and white of a summer sky for cabinets and appliances, adds a few bursts of sunshine in bright yellow cushions, and shows off a prize-winning garden on the walls and ceiling. It's a simple recipe that appeals to everyone in the family, even on the busiest mornings. The adjacent yard and garden are great, but even when the weather is gloomy or chilly, the flower-strewn setting indoors will naturally lift your mood. Key to the look is the colorful, botanically inspired wallcovering. This kind of design appeals to orderly types as well as free spirits, thanks to the latticelike grid that encloses each flower specimen. Whatever your style, if you're going to cover the walls and ceiling with a pattern, make it a design you really love.

A modern kitchen gets a soft, whimsical look, thanks to Wedgwood blue cabinets and the surprising use of botanical wallcovering on the ceiling. Zingy yellow breakfast-chair cushions add an extra dash of cheer. Interior designer: Joseph P. Horan.

A merry mix of floral and geometric prints in a scheme of red, pink, white, and green brings a romantic air to this breakfast nook. Pretty chairs and an ornate garden table of wrought iron and glass establish a nostalgic, outdoor look.
Manufacturer: Seabrook Wallcoverings.

Here's a savvy way to create garden-style drama in a small room: Paint the walls a rich color, then paint lattice from the local home center white, and nail it up. Easier still, look for faux lattice or trellis-pattern wallcovering. Boost the romance with pretty, beribboned botanical prints.
Interior designer: Sande Chernett.

Chic and Charming

To CREATE A SOPHISTICATED garden look, pick a combination of two or three colors, and stick with it. Any green plus white is a natural winner; green, white, and a flower color of your choice is another sure bet. To keep the look from becoming too sweet, skip the floral prints altogether in favor of latticework, trellises, or picket-fence patterns. Another idea is to pair your favorite floral print with a tailored stripe, check, or plaid in matching colors. Complete your airy look with a clever mix of wooden chairs and a glass-top table. In these rooms, chairs in the early modern style of Thonet Bentwood pair with a white iron-and-glass dining table; Napoleon-back chairs (named for the French general's hat) cozy up to a little glass-top, iron breakfast table.

Brought in on a Breeze

OPEN FLORAL PATTERNS that feature sprays of flowers or leaves widely spaced against a pale background have an inherently casual charm. Where dense, dark-hued designs can be formal and even a bit overwhelming, pale, scattered florals give the area visual breathing room. If your taste runs to contemporary designs, stylized flowers in virtually any color combination are available. If traditional or vintage style is more your cup of tea, look for prints depicting flowers and foliage that naturally grow in tendrils or on vines. Ivy, brambly raspberries and blackberries, grapevines, clematis, climbing roses, and other favorites lend themselves to airy, twining patterns. Repeat the motif with silk or real vines at windows, above cupboards, or in other strategic areas around the room. For a crisp, stylish look, confine yourself to two or three colors; for a relaxed, heirloom look, leave your real vintage furnishings in whatever colors you find them.

Left: *A high-ceilinged dining alcove inspired this airy, fantasy gazebo theme. Blouson valances, deeply shirred and charmingly trimmed, repeat the twining ivy pattern of the wallcovering. Above them, garlands of silk ivy vines fill the alcove ceiling. Green-painted Windsor chairs carry the color theme with comfort.* Above: *Iron wire baskets like these let air circulate better around fresh food, from exotic pomegranates to humble potatoes. With their wooden handles, the baskets look great on their own, too.* Source: *Ballard Designs.*

Purple-red berries, grapes, and small blossoms grace this open-pattern wallcovering and its companion, a more dense and colorful still-life border. An old table and chairs in punchy yellow, red, and green are surprising choices that evoke an extra-relaxed feeling. Manufacturer: Seabrook Wallcoverings.

Distinctively Different

P AINTS, WALLCOVERINGS, AND fabrics can create rooms with entirely different moods,
from subtle and sophisticated to countrified and
colorful. These two rooms contain similar elements but portray unique looks. The dressy taupe
setting makes a case for eclectic savoir faire:
Chairs covered in an obviously modern print are
right at home with the classical print that tops
the table and covers the walls. The smooth flow
of related tones lends a soothing, graceful feeling
that encourages guests to linger long after coffee.
In a whole different mood, the casual country
setting employs dramatic color contrasts, fun
wallpaper motifs, and a general air of impromptu
hospitality served up with cheer. Color is the
most compelling element in any design scheme,
so pick a hue you'd love to live with. Then pull
two or three other colors that blend or contrast
to create the whole look.

Left: *Perhaps inspired by old garden statuary, the gently weathered
shades of taupe, ivory, and gray in this room produce a quietly
romantic effect. The piecework tablecloth makes a unique, tailored
statement without jarring the mood.* Manufacturer: Stroheim &
Romann. Above: *Native to the Mediterranean, rosemary is grown
the world over. Place one or two terra-cotta pots of the herb, real or
silk, on the kitchen or dining room table for a refreshing centerpiece of green.* Manufacturer: NDI.

Rosy fruits and flowers on a dark espresso background establish a striking country setting. High-contrast patterns like this demand attention, so solid colors work best for the other elements. These owners used the expected white, but then shook up the look with a table and cabinets in lively spring green. Manufacturer: Waverly.

Appetizing Color

CANTALOUPE, strawberry ice cream, butterscotch, peach sorbet: Some of our most appetizing flavors are appealing colors, too. Tints of pink, peach, and gold lend warmth to any room, especially one that faces north or east, but they really come into their own in a kitchen or dining room. Add rich cream to these sherbet tints and you make a fresh, inviting combination that is warm and romantic. Take a tip from the decorators: Instead of chilly, stark white, choose a white with a hint of peach or blush to team with these warm tones. They will blend more gracefully. Most wood tones look good with peachy hues as they share golden undertones. With pink, you can use wood tones for warmth or go a bit cooler by using hunter green and dove gray as neutrals. Either palette gives you the ingredients for delectable dining.

Left: *A delicate tracery of stylized grapevines adds a pretty touch to this casually elegant dining room. A palette of peaches and cream is balanced by strong gold-and-brown tones that give the space stability. Swaddled chairs, a whimsical chandelier, and crisply trimmed curtains convey the feeling of a romantic getaway.*

Opposite: *A fresh burst of pink gives a dining spot a romantic, vivacious feeling. The beauty of this treatment is that it's easy to accomplish when you run short of time: Just tie a linen tablecloth or a crisp cotton sheet around each chair.*

Fun in Good Taste

This clever carrot pot brimming with vegetables will give your kitchen counter or table loads of garden-fresh color all year long. Manufacturer: Natural Decorations, Inc. (NDI)

KITCHENS AND DINING ROOMS are where we prepare and enjoy our favorite fruits, vegetables, and flowers. Whether they come from our own gardens or the local produce and flower markets, we love to decorate these rooms with garden motifs of all kinds. Look beyond the classic fruit and floral arrangements our mothers relied on and discover fresh ways to bring the outdoors in. The quickest method is to change your printed fabrics—from pot holders to place mats—to prints that celebrate your garden favorites. Pick some zesty red tomatoes, sweet purple violets, or whatever you like. If you're up for a bit of redecorating, wallcoverings and coordinating borders are beautiful and sophisticated. For the kitchen, washable wallcoverings are pretty and practical. If you're going for a renovation, colorful ceramic and porcelain tiles can make your garden passion a lasting one.

Lion's-head motifs have sent an elegant message since medieval times, indoors or out. This bronze planter is a handsome way to show off your prize specimen plants. Source: Wisteria.

Stone is a luxury as well as an entirely natural addition to your interior landscape. This nostalgic, farmhouse-style sink is hand carved from natural Travertine marble and enriched with leaves in bas-relief on the apron. Manufacturer: Artistic Tile.

Here's a distinctive way to add a garden view to any room: Reproduction landscape plans from Renaissance Italy, decoupaged onto fiberboard for easy display. It's charming as a mock window over a door or as a piece of art above a desk or chest. Source: Ballard Designs.

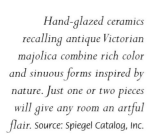

Hand-glazed ceramics recalling antique Victorian majolica combine rich color and sinuous forms inspired by nature. Just one or two pieces will give any room an artful flair. Source: Spiegel Catalog, Inc.

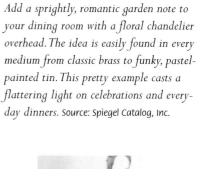

Add a sprightly, romantic garden note to your dining room with a floral chandelier overhead. The idea is easily found in every medium from classic brass to funky, pastel-painted tin. This pretty example casts a flattering light on celebrations and every-day dinners. Source: Spiegel Catalog, Inc.

This Tiffany-style buffet lamp features a "Carolina Jasmine" motif of winsome golden blossoms on a candle-light-yellow background. In artful detail, more blooms entwine the base, finished in rich capitol bronze. The lamp is a stately 29½ inches tall. A coordinating floor lamp is also available. Source: Quoizel.

Floral sprays and bouquets on wallcoverings and upholstery are the stuff romantic decorating schemes are made of. Jewel-tone backgrounds and vivid flowers that share a color scheme look lovely. Manufacturer: Sanderson.

Charming citrus-fruit tiles recall details found in medieval scenes but are as fresh as any contemporary sketch. Designs like these will be as appealing years from now as they are today: Just what you'd want in a product that can last as long as your house. Manufacturer: Walker Zanger.

Blooming Living Rooms, Home Offices & Dens

Aged and weathered pots, planters, topiary frames, and garden tools bring romance to a room by recalling generations of flowers that have gone before. Play with these simple, architectural shapes to create a tablescape or mantel display that evokes your love of gardening in a sophisticated way.

SINCE ANCIENT TIMES, lavish displays of flowers and fruits have brought the beauty of gardens into our homes. Whether you're shopping for the living room, family room, home office, or den, you'll find a world of furnishings to express garden style—your way. Establish your garden motif in living rooms and family rooms with upholstered pieces in fabrics depicting flowers and greenery. When redecorating, choose your fabric first and paint last. It's much easier to custom mix paint to match a fabric than it is to find a fabric that matches a paint chip. Accessorize with floral and other garden-inspired pieces, such as weathered urns. Group together vignettes that suggest outdoor settings, or try an array of flowered antique plates above an orchid in a cachepot. When it comes to decorating your home office, you can escape the spirit-sapping, institutional feeling with flower power. Go beyond the usual desktop vase of cut flowers to create a total nature-loving environment. Ensure physical comfort with adequate glare-free lighting and computer furniture that's ergonomic (designed for the human body). Then, enhance emotional comfort with a fresh garden color scheme, real wood furniture, natural accessories, and a landscape or floral painting. With garden style, your home office can become a tranquil environment for concentration and inspiration.

Dreamscape Remembered

IF YOU LIKE YOUR LIVING ROOM and family room spaces to be more neutral and urbane, consider the alternative shown here. A magical, elusive quality about this room makes you want to explore it, little by little. This is garden style taken to its sophisticated, eclectic limit. The key is an eye for wonderful finds plus a fearless approach to mixing them together. The result is a stunningly unique take on garden inspiration. For starters, the bronze silk draperies are traditionally elegant, but the leaf-embellished sheers are as modern and playful as a Calder mobile. Beyond the leaves, this garden has the sun in the sunburst wall mirror, water in a massive copper fountain, and lots of flowers, from live orchid plants to the floral rug. The effect is dreamlike and utterly soothing.

Above: Beautifully gilded and hand-decorated, a neoclassical cabinet looks graceful as well as imposing. Art deco artwork on the wall and table capture a mood that is sleekly stylized as well as a passionate paean to nature. Right: A classically styled antique chaise and an interestingly textured window seat acquire elegance from trimmed bolster pillows. A huge copper "water wall" fountain has the presence of modern art but creates an Asian-inspired sense of peacefulness.

Graceful old bay windows would look lovely with any window treatment, but these gauzy sheers, embellished with colorful leaf cutouts, are pure magic. Live white orchid plants massed at the windows enhance the graceful feeling. A modern sunburst mirror and a beautifully embroidered floral rug add to the garden message. Interior designer: Stacey Lapuk.

Enchanted Bowers

W HETHER YOU'RE WORKING with a spacious room or a small area, you can layer on romantic, sophisticated garden style with some time-proven strategies. You'll need a focal point, one wonderful element that will visually organize the space and draw attention. It may be a big, fabulous piece of furniture, perhaps hand-painted or filled with special finds, or it could be a large, wonderfully framed window. Other elements fan out or move forward from your focal point, repeating colors, lines, and/or motifs. These rooms—one big and airy, one tiny and cozy—use the patterns made by louvers, bricks, curly woven wicker, and other shapely elements to create subtle layers of interest. Against a confection palette of peach and ivory, wicker in shades from honey to ebony adds more levels of eye-appeal.

Above: When you have a small spot like this, why not create a pocket paradise? A narrow window alcove gets the royal treatment, thanks to tall white wood louvers crowned with a fan louver and the beautifully designed pediment and flanking columns in front. Interior designer: Barbara Ostrom & Associates. Far Right: A glorious, hand-painted armoire with a deep peach interior inspired this sunroom's dreamy color scheme. The brick walls, given an unusual green-gold color, seem to shimmer like sun-dappled leaves. Overhead, a trompe l'oeil conservatory ceiling brings more leafy motifs indoors. Interior designer: Michael Murdolo/Barbara Ostrom & Associates.

Above: Curly willow branches add interest to this arrangement of pink and white roses and green foliage. The decorative, footed vase with an unusual square shape repeats the simple color scheme, enhancing the overall look of the flowers. Manufacturer: NDI.

Home Office Elegance

IF YOUR HOME OFFICE is equipped with the latest electronics but furnished with castoffs, resolve to give yourself the perks you deserve. Millions of Americans are home office-based, and manufacturers are responding with great-looking, well-priced office furniture that blends in beautifully with the rest of your home. If space is tight, look into ingenious home office armoires that put a whole workstation into traditional-looking cabinetry. If you have more room, choose desks that let you spread out. You can adapt an antique writing desk, make a custom desk with a work surface set on pedestals of your choice, or choose a wood executive desk, available in a wide range of prices. Whatever your style, get the best ergonomic office chair you can afford, plan for plenty of light, and make sure your wrists will rest at a comfortable level if you use a computer more than occasionally.

Pure white millwork sparkles against deep blue-gray walls in this pristine home office. A mixture of modern and traditional furniture is focused on the artful desk made of heavy, tempered glass atop two neoclassical columns. Easy-care, live plants thrive near the windows while fresh-cut flowers delight from across the room. Interior designer: Marilee Schemp/ Design 1.

A sheltered window trimmed in garden green paint casts sunlight onto a pretty writing desk. Desks like this have been in use for around 300 years, but you can use one with a modern laptop as long as your chair height allows you to type at a comfortable level.

Romantic Drama

I F THE PHRASE "PINK AND BLACK" makes you think of Elvis and 1950s style, think again. This room is retro all right, but it hearkens back to the mid-1800s. Spun-sugar pink weaves its sentimental spell on everyone who enters this living room, and all succumb happily. The secret? Shots of intense rose, strong patterns, and lots of sharp, shiny black. First, take care of the hard surfaces: a glossy, black-finished wood floor plus ebonized and black-lacquer furniture, both popular in England during the 1800s. Then, create a rich, voluptuous look with a woven rug and a chintz fabric, both with intensely colored blooms that virtually pop from their deep black backgrounds. To keep it from becoming too much of a good thing, these owners went off-script with a dazzle of parrot tulips in yellow as well as deep and pale pink. Many rooms are cozy and inviting, but this one is downright seductive.

Above: The black toile tray table, needlepoint footstool, iron plate stand, and black enamel-and-gold frames carry the high-contrast color scheme throughout the room. An elaborately carved fireplace mantel, painted white, keeps the overall effect light, not oppressive. **Right:** *Peruvian and Stargazer lilies, snapdragons, and other garden beauties make a vivacious statement. Cue flower colors to your room's palette, or choose a dominant color (such as the rose red in this arrangement) and experiment with accent hues. For example, use blue irises instead of yellow Peruvian lilies.* **Manufacturer:** NDI.

Bold, traditional floral patterns link the pale pink walls and the deep black floor with energy and elegance. To make the most of graceful ceiling-height windows, valances are made of the same fabric as the draperies. Maximizing the room's height and using pale-tint walls visually expand the space.

Right: A Gothic Revival-style chair is just one of the distinctive items in this magical setting. A mantelpiece, sans fireplace, holds an interesting array of artifacts and an ivy plant. More plants rise from the floor, showcased with classically inspired pedestals and urns. Even with a nearly neutral palette, the look is rich.

Trompe l'oeil is used here to fabulous effect. A contemporary living room accented with gazing balls and a few other fun garden elements opens to a vista on one wall. Past the faux open door, a clump of pale poppies leads the eye to a gazebo beyond. Talk about a focal point!
Interior designer: Gary Crain.

Cream of the Crop

PLAYFUL AND SOPHISTICATED, these areas show how fresh and inspiring a mostly white palette can be. To your favorite creamy tone add black, deep green, and a few glints of gold, and you have a sleek, inherently dramatic look. In a nearly no-color setting, shape is everything, so seek out wonderfully curved upholstered pieces, architecturally interesting lamps and tables, and accents in a mix of textures: smooth and shiny, rough and matte. In these rooms, black wrought iron, braided rattan, silky chintz, terra-cotta, marble, stone, gold leaf, and silvery chrome make the statement with relaxed artistry. A few master touches, like the knockout trompe l'oeil scene and the Gothic chair, focus these rooms. The deep green of specimen plants, each with its own graceful lines, adds the warmth of living, growing things.

Blithe Spirit

CITY HOMES, whether they be renovated mansions, charming little condos, or something in between, seem especially appreciative of garden style. Against all the cool, urban grayness, a few bright spots of flower colors and green stand out vividly. And when you come out of a winter's dusk into springtime-color rooms like these, filled with real flowers and floral images, the effect is even more precious. Create an inviting living room where nothing matches but everything goes together. English, French, and Italian inspirations work delightfully, and the mood is one of gracious welcome. To round out the look, beautiful live plants—tall blue delphinium, lush pink hydrangea—echo colorful fabric images of pansies, asters, and other simple favorites. When you need a break from the daily grind, a space like this can be just the ticket.

Warm-toned ranunculus, daisies, and zinnias team with cool-toned cornflowers, delphinium, scabiosa, and hydrangea for a nicely balanced, lush arrangement. A few stray blossoms peep out at the top to avoid a static pincushion look. A footed black base lends formal importance, whereas a basket would create a casual effect. Manufacturer: NDI.

A fabulously carved wood mantel and mirror frame carry the floral theme in garlands, branches, and birds. Next to this eye-catching antique, a voluptuously padded chaise in sprightly blue offers an enticing invitation to curl up and read.

A cheerful mix of cornflower blue, coral, yellow, and green gives this distinctive setting a fresh feeling. Bas-relief columns and classically draped swags enhance the stature of the windows, but the effect is eased with simple café-length sheers.

Tropical Punch

TROPICALLY INSPIRED DECORATING can take many forms, from the simplicity of a beach cabana to the lavishness of a royal dwelling. For furnishings, you might start with reproductions of British and French colonial styles, or outdoor furniture in wicker, rattan, or wrought iron. For major upholstered pieces, choose a distinctive, tropical-flower pattern and take colors from it for your solid-color cushions and accent fabrics (or vice versa). Complete the exotic setting with decorative furnishings and other treasures from your favorite warm-climate cultures and civilizations. Indonesia, Polynesia, Hawaii, the Indian subcontinent, the Caribbean, and South America are some places to explore for decorating inspirations. Whether you like a Victorian layered look, a simple "island paradise" look, or something in between, be sure to add a few live, tropical, flowering plants to perfume the room and bring the whole look together.

Left: *Luscious coral, taupe, and ivory create a sophisticated take on a tropical scheme. A mix of subtly textured solids with a smooth, chintz-like print looks great against the pronounced texture of the woven-fiber furniture.* Manufacturer: Stroheim & Romann. Above: *Asian-influenced, roomy oval baskets have a pleasing shape and texture that adds impact to your décor. Use them nested as a decorative element or separately to keep clutter under control. They are crafted of woven wicker with sturdy wooden handles for natural appeal.* Source: Coldwater Creek.

An alcove with barley-twist columns and neo-Gothic trim makes a grand frame for a floral sofa and set of botanical prints. The scheme of dark green, coral, and peach gets even more punch from the mix of whimsically ornate furnishings. Interior designer: Barbara Ostrom & Associates.

This room uses a real tree branch entwined with a vine of silk ivy. It makes a winsome drapery rod to hold plain, pale draperies that don't distract your eye from the view out-doors. A charming twig baker's rack holds small potted plants, and a stone rabbit keeps the door open to the breeze.

Just the Right Touch

Wire plant forms and a weathered urn and pots make a simple, yet evocative mantel display in this unpretentious garden room. A spare blue folding chair and a plump beige rattan chair prove that in a monochromatic scheme shape is everything.

F YOUR IDEA OF GARDEN STYLE is on the simple, rustic side, you can still have a space that's chic and distinctive. The secret is to make sure every piece in your home is functional or beautiful or both. In this sort of setting, housekeeping clutter is almost nonexistent. On the other hand, every architectural element, piece of furniture, and accessory stands out, so each has to be special. Luckily, "special" doesn't mean expensive. Import shops, resale stores, and flea markets are great places to find sleek or sentimental pieces with shapes that stand out against uncluttered back-grounds. If you're torn between two great furniture finds, choose the one that's more functional and comfortable. If the tie is between several decorative accessories, pick the one with the finer workmanship or more interesting shape. You'll be able to live with them longer, and you'll enjoy the freedom that simple chic delivers.

Renaissance Masterpiece

ROMPE L'OEIL, the French phrase for "trick the eye," has transformed ordinary walls since the invention of three-point perspective drawing during the Renaissance. Today, trompe l'oeil effects are available in wallcoverings and stencils, or they can be drawn freehand by artists. Trompe l'oeil is a realistic painting style, but the settings and elements most often painted are the stuff of fantasy. So if you'd like your home office to be housed in a medieval Gothic abbey overlooking Tuscan fields, you can have it. If you'd like to look at a gorgeous vase of your favorite flowers and never have to change the water, you can have that, too. If your home office is in a small room or in a basement with minimal natural light, you'll be happiest with an outdoor vista. With trompe l'oeil, your own personal paradise can be the place where you are right now.

A Gothic-style cabinet and a floral-upholstered French chair make a romantic statement in this artist's studio, but the fantastical trompe l'oeil flower arrangement is what really catches the eye. Re-creating a centuries-old tradition, this elaborate, realistic painting of bleeding-hearts and delphinium in a vase offers inspiration that never fades.

Opposite: The masterful illusion in this study focuses on an arched nook looking out into a stone courtyard and the remnants of a formal garden beyond. The effect is carried onto other walls and even the ceiling. Who says a quiet, contemplative room can't make you smile?

Accent on Nature

WHETHER YOU'RE FURNISHING an opulent 18th-century living room or a modern minimalist office, garden-inspired touches add timeless grace and vitality to your space. To get the look, start with live plants and fresh flowers wherever possible. Be sure plants are great specimens in superb health and the flowers work with your color scheme. Expand the effect with actual garden accents in real or faux stone and cast iron. These can make plants serve as the focal point or stand in for more formal statuary, instantly relaxing any room. The same goes for baskets used to hold just about anything. A few pieces of wicker, rattan, and bamboo furniture add a natural feeling that can be romantic or tropically exotic. Upholstery, rugs, and decorative pillows with leafy or floral subjects give a boost to the garden look. Easiest of all accents, landscape or still-life paintings can show instant garden inspiration.

A leafy, scrolled charmer, the base of this whimsical wrought-iron end table is washed in lively green. A tempered glass top, 24 inches in diameter, is practical and visually airy, adding the perfect grace note for a small area. Source: Spiegel Catalog, Inc.

Bring the soothing quality of gently falling water to your home office or any room with this handsome desktop fountain. Water trickles over a natural slate wall onto river rocks in a copper basin that conceals a recirculating pump. Source: Smith & Hawken.

Romantic and robust, this West Indies sofa evokes the rich heritage of the islands and the elegant influences of the colonial era. Dark wood-tone or jewel-tone wicker looks substantial enough for indoor use and makes a whimsical addition to a formal, 19th-century-style room. Manufacturer: Summer Classics.

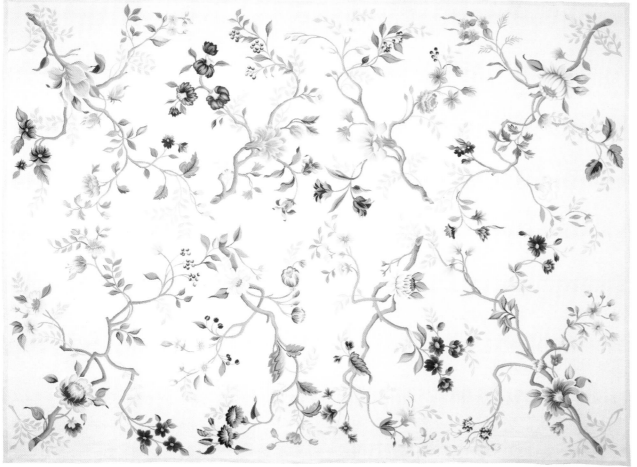

Luscious red cherries fairly pop out of this finely crafted needlepoint pillow. Manufacturer: Michaelian and Kohlberg.

The botanically inspired "Branches" rug, in pure wool, continues an artistry that never goes out of favor. This design features artfully worked flowers in Wedgwood blue, violet, yellow, and garnet red on a pale yellow ground. Manufacturer: Asmara, Inc.

Like a find from an old New Orleans apartment, this shabby-genteel wall sconce hints of romances past with its delicately tinted iron flowers and leaves. Source: Ballard Designs.

Part of the Chelsea Collection, this hand-woven rattan chair was inspired by the beautiful tortoiseshell bamboo furniture found in London's Brighton Pavilion at the turn of the 20th century. However, it is much more durable. Manufacturer: PierceMartin.

Bathroom Oases

WATER AND GARDENS go together naturally, and garden images are a great way to add visual warmth and softness to the bath. Nothing dispels a cold, utilitarian feeling like ferns, water lilies, ivy, old-fashioned roses, or retro tropical hibiscus. Elegant, nostalgic, or fun, garden motifs are available in water-resistant vinyl wallcoverings and paintable stencils, so you can make a splash with your favorite looks. Play off neutral-hued bath fixtures with color in towels, rugs, and accessories. Some manufacturers offer coor- dinated sets, but don't go overboard with one pattern or your bath will look small and cluttered. If you love a strong pattern on the walls, pick up one or two of its hues in solid-color towels and rugs. For painted walls, consider the chic yellow-green of baby lettuce or a skin-flattering petal pink or peach. Paint a white lattice pattern over it for fun, and use flower-motif cabinet hardware. If your bath enjoys a fair amount of natural light, display a Boston fern, orchid, or other moisture-loving plant. Big or small, today's bath is just the place to create your own tropical paradise.

Opposite: *This restful oasis is no mirage. A garden of beautiful, healthy houseplants surrounds a whirlpool tub with a waterfall spout, creating an inviting, luxurious bathroom retreat.* Interior designer: Accent on Design. Above: *Serenely at home in a bath that's Asian, traditional European, or modern, the graceful "Petals" glass sink bowl seems to have drifted down from a flowering tree.* Manufacturer: Jacuzzi Whirlpool Bath.

An all-white bath could be chilly, but not in this case, thanks to a subtly artful trompe l'oeil treatment. From the cracks of aged white stone walls, moss emerges and blue morning glories twine.

Tranquility Found

Bathrooms from the 1930s or earlier can be easier to refurbish than later models, because they're often more gracefully designed. Whether you have a genuine old bath or a new one that you want to look old, traditional garden style can be a refreshing option. Start with white, rectangular "subway" tiles instead of modern squares for the walls, or create faux stone tiles with trompe l'oeil. Use small, classic, hexagonal tiles in white or black and white for the floor and traditional pedestal sinks and other fixtures, which are found everywhere from design centers to home centers. Add a wallcovering or wall treatment that summons a green scene or a favorite flower. Cool tones of nature-loving green and blue are traditional favorites in the bath, so they're perfect for any garden scheme. Add a few personal treasures, a plant or two in old cachepots, the modern magic of running water, and relax!

Opposite: A soothing wraparound watercolor on the wall recalls elegant scenes that decorated walls in the 18th century. Here, it transports a bather far away from modern stress. Creamy white throughout the room enhances the serenity, and dark antique accents add richness.

Exotic and sophisticated, this bath features an extraordinary tile mural of tropical split-leaf philodendrons, dragonflies, and other natural charmers. If you favor small frogs, chameleons, snails, or other garden wildlife, they'd make witty accents in a bath like this. One large leaf serves as a light sconce. Interior designer: Anjum Razvi.

Simple Forms

Opposite: *The ambience of this bath clearly manifests with the sinuous forms of vines and the varied shapes of leaves repeated throughout the space. Made of both natural and artificial elements, they create interest in a way that's soothing yet modern.*

A ROOM CAN DISPLAY A GARDEN environment without using flower colors. Leaves, branches, vines, and grasses have inherently interesting shapes and work better than frilly florals for many color schemes. Asian, African, Arts & Crafts, modern, and eclectic settings, among others, take easily to these striking natural forms. To keep the forms in the forefront, use neutral tones ranging from pristine white to rich, dark brown, plus a bit of deep green. Then add texture with wicker, rattan, vines, baskets, grapevine wreaths, and the like. Look for wood, stone, granite, and other naturally patterned materials, and consider decorative tiles with natural motifs as accents. These two master baths—one coolly serene, one warmly exotic—show how appealing this approach can be.

Romance of the Rose

ROSE-RED, WHITE, AND green make a beautiful, classic color scheme for a traditional bath filled with grand gestures and romantic elements galore. For those who think bountiful baths are a modern convenience, it's fun to recall that in the old days, when "the facilities" were housed in outbuildings, an affluent family might very well have enjoyed one or more rooms like this for bathing and dressing. A big bathroom can handle the strong patterns and deep, contrasting garden hues these owners love. If your bathroom is smaller, you might consider a lighter, softer tint, but if you really love red (or any other strong flower color), why not go for the full-strength version? Whatever accent color you choose, you can't go wrong with soft ivory-white and sage or hunter green as the background shades in your traditional scheme. Roses come in lots of hues, so pick your favorite!

Antique or just antique-inspired, a lovely, hand-decorated vanity and mirror make a natural focal point in any bath. When the overall look is unabashedly traditional, a subtly embellished piece works best with a lushly flowered wallcovering.

A big bath can take more than one grand gesture. Here, bold harlequin diamonds deck a vintage-style slipper tub. A picture-pretty, skirted slipper chair adds another special touch. Rose-strewn wallcovering and matching window treatments complete the lavish look.

Botanical floral tiles, in the form of wallcovering borders, bracket the freely scattered poppies, irises, tiger lilies, and other garden favorites in this chic and charming bath. A coordinating shower curtain adds a more brisk pattern and verve. Small pieces of freestanding furniture lend presence and practicality.
Manufacturer: Seabrook Wallcoverings.

Inspired by antique bathtubs, a luxurious new tub enjoys pride of place for its great lines and pretty floral-chintz base. Coordinating floral fixtures and tiles dazzle against English cream and hunter green walls. Manufacturer: Kohler.

Flowers for the Picking

FLORAL-PATTERN ENGLISH CHINA has captured hearts for hundreds of years. So have botanical prints of flowers, those realistic and colorful illustrations that grew along with scientific observation in the 1700s and 1800s. These traditional favorites show up in all kinds of inventive ways. Porcelain bath fixtures take naturally to the art of painted floral designs, and they're so pretty you don't need much else in the way of decoration. In fact, from a decorating perspective, patterned fixtures are like patterned upholstery—plain walls set them off best. If you're not ready to take the plunge into patterned fixtures, try floral-pattern ceramic or porcelain tiles as a border around a mirror. Botanically inspired wallcoverings are another way to get a handsome floral look that stands the test of time. Naturally colored and rendered, these carefully detailed images are as delightful now as ever before.

Delicate Impressions

To bring a gentle garden air to any room, swaddle the walls and ceiling in flower-sprigged wallpaper. These two baths illustrate the subtle charm of this simple technique. If your bath is a made-over bedroom or part of a big new master suite, it will feel cozier with an all-over wallcovering pattern. If your bath is the standard five feet-by-seven feet size, it will look dramatic instead of skimpy. Either way, with these backgrounds, it takes only a few special accents to pull the look together. If there's room for one or two pieces of real furniture, choose curvy, rounded shapes for sensual appeal and safety. A slipper chair, plumply upholstered stool, cabriole-leg table, or classic urn make an elegant statement. Ivory and soft green serenely set off floral tints, and a bit of gold or silver lends a glamorous finish.

An enchanting wallcovering of lilacs wraps this small, traditional bath in European charm. The oversize, neoclassical garden urn gives greenery good access to sunshine. Simple white sheers draped from a rod of black scrolling leaves balance the opulence of the ornate gilded mirror and velvet upholstered stool. Interior designer: Melinda Kuehne.

What could be more comfy than a lovely upholstered chair to welcome you after a soak in an old-fashioned, claw-foot bathtub? This charming room's gentle tints of ivory, pink, and green underscore the vintage English-garden look. Architect/interior designer: Quinn Evans Architects.

Tropical Fantasy

A STRONG THEME CAN BE captivating, depending on how the presentation is handled. In this spacious bath, the balance of vivid elements and subtle backgrounds is managed so gracefully that the look could easily translate to an average-size bath. The sandy yellow-and-white color scheme is warm, comfortable, and inviting. A botanical wall-covering of varieties of ferns adds visual interest in a quiet way. Against this appealing background, bright custom-tile murals of jungle parrots stand out with the richness of oil paintings. Wisely, these owners confined the decorative gestures to just a few areas, letting the large mirror and overall scale of the room add a dramatic sense of expansiveness. The same tricks, such as a striking focal point supported by room-enlarging mirrors, can also give a smaller bath real presence.

This spacious bath would be impressive all by itself, but the wonderful custom-tile scenes of tropical parrots launch the room into the realm of the spectacular. The simple color scheme lets the larger custom mural take center stage.

A bamboo chair with a lively tropical print works nicely with the generously scaled vanity in this jungle-inspired bath. Ferns deck the walls, including the half-height partition enclosing the commode, a thoughtful touch for any bath.

A sprightly border in periwinkle, leaf green, and lime gives a fresh lift to a mostly pure-white bath. A claw-foot tub and bead-board paneling bring traditional elements to the mix. The etched-glass cabinet and leafy wallcovering reinforce the playful, modern mood.
Manufacturer: Brewster Wallcovering.

Watercolor Effects

N THE BATH, IT'S smart to use white for installed products like floors, fixtures, and cabinets. After all, white goes with everything and visually expands space. But past the practical side, a plain white bath needs a boost. Luckily, it takes very little to create whatever scheme or mood you like. These two bathrooms have traditionally styled cabinets and contemporary fixtures but really need more. Garden style comes to the rescue, drenching ho-hum rooms with luscious color and sprightly patterns. One palette uses white, periwinkle, and lime; the other uses these colors and adds magenta, but both evoke a sense of instant springtime. To get these refreshing results, grab a gallon of paint or a few rolls of vinyl wall-covering and go for it. Then live it up by adding towels and bath accessories in coordinating colors.

Sponged-effect walls in periwinkle with a border of magenta water lilies and green lily pads are all the art this white bath needs. Towels, bath rug, and accents in periwinkle and magenta balance the green of live plants. Manufacturer: Brewster Wallcovering.

Playing Favorites

Gᴀʀᴅᴇɴ ꜱᴛʏʟᴇ ʀᴜɴꜱ the gamut from wildly romantic to crisply tailored. Since walls occupy the largest area in the room, make sure they set the scene right. A combination of wallcovering and bead-board is a traditional favorite that's especially at home in a cottage garden-style bath. If the room is small, create visual flow by painting the bead-board the background color of the wallcovering (assuming it's not too dark). If the room is large, boost excitement by painting the bead-board one of the accent colors instead. Another option is to deck your walls in garden-motif tiles. You can use tiles where you wouldn't use paper and wallboard, but they are a rather permanent solution—be sure you really love the design or pick a fairly conservative pattern. Green and white lattice or trellis motifs are ideally versatile, and you can build up the floral look with accessories.

Left: A lattice pattern in taupe and soft white sets a quietly elegant garden mood in the bath. A simple, contrasting-pattern border defines the mirror and adds interest elsewhere. Woven baskets holding potted flowers echo the trellis motif. Interior designer: Country Floors.

Opposite: An unusual lilac-strewn wallpaper with a golden-yellow background lends an aged and sunny air to this spacious bath. Honey pine and terra-cotta enhance the feeling of warmth. A lightly scaled baker's rack shows off garden-inspired, vintage keepsakes and offers convenient open storage.

Flowery Sentiments

I F YOU'VE INHERITED an old or ordinary bathroom and don't have the option of changing the cabinets and fixtures, don't fret. While some decorating schemes depend on everything being just so, garden style is as forgiving as it is charming. If you pick a frisky, modern scheme, you can draw attention to paintbox colors and funky accessories for a lift. But if your preference is something on the more traditional side, why not bring on the romance with a fanciful Victorian setting? On the walls, paint some ribbons and flowers like the charming "tussy-mussie" bouquets of Queen Victoria's time, or use a wallpaper with this sweet motif. Add the romance of ornately framed mirrors, elegant traditional lighting, and rich, vintage accessories, such as treasured family photos and silk floral accents. A pretty little chair or lavishly upholstered vanity stool is an important addition: It gives even a tiny bath the feeling of a real room with special comforts.

Left: *A charming trompe l'oeil portrait of a little girl in a garden beckons from just beyond this romantic bath. A fantastic Venetian-glass mirror and a black-and-gilt, papier-mâché Victorian chair put the vintage sink in glamorous company.*

Opposite: *Sumptuous mauve moiré satin plus sea-foam blue and ivory make a pretty Victorian statement in this feminine suite. Lavish floral bouquets are an important part of the delightful look that gives each nook the appeal of a garden vignette.*

Showers of Flowers

GARDEN-MOTIF BATH FIXTURES, fittings, fabrics, tiles, and accessories are more plentiful than ever, so you can easily find the look you desire. From a decorating perspective, you'll want to decide ahead if you prefer a color scheme based on a few shades, such as yellow plus blue or burgundy/rose/pale pink, or on a full range of shades, such as colors seen in a cottage garden. If you choose decorated fixtures or tiles, these are relatively permanent choices, so select them first. For maximum flexibility, you may want to balance a special print with coordinated solid colors. Keep in mind that it's always easier to find solid colors to coordinate with a print than vice versa. When you want a change later, just change the solid you're emphasizing, and give an old favorite a fresh new look.

In the 1600s, tulips were a passion bordering on mania in the Netherlands. Your passion will be equally ignited by these tiles, inspired by 17th-century botanical drawings. Part of a suite that includes major fixtures and accessories, the tiles depict tulips in loving detail on a crackled white background. Manufacturer: Kohler.

Poppies are exotic, yet as familiar as Grandmother's perennial garden, so these flowers work in almost any style, from Asian to French Country. Against the chic neutral tones of these towels, the dainty red blooms stand out with flair. Manufacturer: Avanti.

Give a small bath a grace note of garden inspiration with this lattice-and-scrollwork gazebo of handmade iron. It's the perfect space-saving storage piece. Source: Ballard Designs.

A pretty, handwoven rattan plant stand with a pair of ruffled-edge baskets recalls grandmother's charming porch furniture. The stand fits anywhere and is light enough to carry by its arched basket handle. Source: Coldwater Creek.

Accent chairs abound, but few can prompt instant smiles as this one does. Full of high-spirited style and delightfully curvy, this West Indies chair of bentwood and wicker melds graceful European designs with tropical island flair. Manufacturer: Summer Classics.

Stash towels in style or lug laundry with flair: These rattan baskets with sturdy wooden frames and handles do the job right. Outside the bath, they're a handsome way to corral toys, garden tools, or anything that benefits from the ventilated design. Source: Ballard Designs.

For breezy, front-porch charm in your garden-style bath, this bead-board storage tower can handily hold towels, bath gels, soaps, and the like. Source: Ballard Designs.

A pampering must for any bath is a soft rug to keep toes cozy. This bamboo-pattern rug in celadon and ivory is a blend of soft cotton and luxurious linen, yet it can be machine washed and dried. Source: Gump's.

Bedroom Bowers

I T'S YOUR BOUDOIR, YOUR NEST, your personal retreat. Your bedroom is the ideal place
to create a romantic garden environment. Start with the bed, which is the room's
focal point and the biggest opportunity to layer on the garden looks. Quilts, sheets,
comforter covers, and decorative toss pillows are all available in cheerful floral prints
or elegantly embroidered floral motifs. But don't overlook ferns and vines, butterflies
and bees, garden animals, and other whimsical garden elements. They'll prevent your
flower motifs from looking too sweet. For tailored punch with garden spirit, contrast
florals with airy, geometric lattice patterns. If your room overlooks a pretty garden,
use simple window treatments for privacy and let the view be the star. A big vanity
mirror opposite the window will help bring the garden in. Keep in mind the mix of
colors and patterns on your bed when you select wall treatments. If the walls are
strongly patterned, let the bed be visually quieter (or vice versa). On a painted wall,
add a simple painted trompe l'oeil garland above the head of your bed, hang a sentimental grapevine heart, or use a section of white picket fence as a whimsical headboard. With garden style, any bedroom feels more serene, romantic, and nurturing.

*If you're lucky enough to
have big, beautiful bedroom
windows overlooking your
gardens, indoor décor can
be simplicity itself. Here, a
vintage-style plant stand gives
sun-loving geraniums an outside view. The vertical stripe
effect of the planter's slats is
mimicked in the cabana-stripe
cushions of a nearby chaise.
What could be more relaxing?*
Manufacturer: Swedish Blonde.

Romantic Allusions

APHRODITE WOULD BE COMPLETELY at home in this frankly feminine boudoir, but thoughtful planning is the secret behind such enchantment. First, the background scheme: tender tints of blush and ivory that wrap the room in serenity. Then, there are the main fabrics, one a pink lattice, the other a pink lattice overlaid with lilies of the valley. Where roses would be the expected choice, lily of the valley, a modest shade flower and a wedding tradition, lends a quirky, endearing quality. Also important is the emphasis on practical comforts, not just pretty gestures. For example, the vanity is positioned so that makeup application is easy, thanks to ample, even light, and the chaise longue adds sublime comfort. Finally, there are magical accents aplenty, such as the Italian, silver-leaf, "grotto" vanity chair and the tall, flowering bougainvillea plants that create the feeling of a garden bower. The result is a lady's retreat of pure enchantment.

Above: *Cherished photos in heirloom silver frames and a vase of roses from the owner's garden keep company with a dainty little fringed-shade lamp. In a setting like this, even a few fresh blooms bring the garden indoors.*

Left: *A French chaise longue imparts glamour anywhere. Piled with pillows, draped with a lightweight, warm mohair throw, and stationed near a table and good sources of light, it's also flawlessly comfortable.*

A dressing table is romantic enough, but when it's draped in pink ribbon lattice and lilies of the valley, it's downright idyllic. The bay windows, lightly dressed in a coordinating pink ribbon lattice fabric and plain white gauze, make a dreamy backdrop. Interior designer: Joseph P. Horan.

An old-fashioned, kidney-shape vanity recalls the glamorous 1930s, and the crown canopy over the quilted bed hearkens back to 18th-century romantic style straight out of a fairy tale. An array of prints, all in the same subtle color scheme of grayed lavender, putty, and green, give the setting an air of quiet, feminine sophistication.

Hints of Spring

WHEN WE THINK OF SPRINGTIME colors, we often think of lavender plus light yellow or the palest spring green. Crocuses, daffodils, hyacinths, and lilacs are favorites from February through May, but these uplifting tints can brighten your rooms all year. Violet and yellow happen to be opposites on the color wheel, so using them together creates a pleasing balance; lavender plus almost any tint of green is fresh and stylish. If you want to use one of these hues alone, keep in mind that lilac, lavender, and related tints of pale violet are cool, receding colors. Lilac can visually expand a small room or give a space with southern or western exposure a cooler feeling. The effect is calming and can be surprisingly sophisticated, depending on the other colors and elements in the space. Whatever the setting, the naturally delicate, springtime tints of violet, yellow, and green work magic in any room—but especially so in a bedroom.

Soft lilac, white, and mauve-pink pillows and throws soften the spare lines of a graceful, black metal daybed in a room painted creamy yellow. A pale lavender screen adorned with handwritten names of flowers lends a casual, artful touch.

Sage Advice

SAGE, THAT INDEFINITE, quietly sophisticated shade of grayed green, makes a serene and ageless background for any room. While brighter, more assertive greens give a youthful, lively look, sage and other soft herbal greens create a quiet, contemplative garden atmosphere that is very soothing. Because sage is a muted tone, it takes well to any setting where you'd like to create an air of antiquity. In the rooms shown here, sage green combines with oyster, light taupe, antique ivory, and a bit of old gold for an effect that's more like texture than color. For a chic update on sage, pair it with lilac or any other tint of violet, from periwinkle to orchid. For a pretty, vintage feeling, use sage with blossom pink or robin's-egg blue; if you like Southwest style, team sage with terra-cotta. Versatile and elegant, sage sets the scene.

Left: Skirted, kidney-shape vanity tables, all the rage from the 1920s to 1950s, lend an aura of glamour to today's boudoir. Look for silver gallery trays and vanity sets at estate sales and resale shops. The essential mirror, an antique, is etched with a floral spray that echoes the wallpaper and drapery motif. Manufacturer: Stroheim & Romann. Above: Dried hydrangeas' interesting flower heads have attained popularity in recent years, but they're no match for the full glory of fresh or faux-fresh blooms. The hydrangeas in this arrangement create a pleasing complementary scheme of red-violet and green. Manufacturer: NDI.

A bedroom under the eaves
has an inherently private
feeling, enhanced by the subtly
coordinated mix of wallcoverings and borders. This austere
room, furnished with rustic
old pieces, gets a lift from a
gauzy bedskirt and a toile
pillow, plus white flowers
everywhere. Mercury-glass
baubles add a bit of glimmer.
Manufacturer: Seabrook
Wallcoverings.

Domestic Tranquility

A cane-inset bergere chair and ottoman give a romantic French accent to this reading corner. Antique handkerchiefs, jewelry, small art prints, and other personal treasures, all carefully framed, create a personal mood.

IN ITS ORIGINAL FORM, VICTORIAN style was rather dark and fussy compared to our tastes now. But there's no denying the homey warmth and frankly sentimental charms of that era, and these are the elements we appreciate. This inviting garden bedroom abounds with pretty airs and pampering touches that would inspire envy in the queen herself. To enhance the spacious feeling, backgrounds are simple except for a few masterful touches, such as the trompe l'oeil flowering vines on the walls. Creating a sense of cozy charm, soft red and ivory fabrics are layered throughout the room, especially on the unusual bed. Lavish draperies, lovely lace pillows, and favorite antique accessories make a richly personal retreat that stands the test of time. The outdoor dining table draped in crisp Battenburg lace carries the Victorian charm outside, making a lovely spot for a private breakfast or tea.

Left: *A tall heirloom-style bed in dark, shining wood is a Victorian-era favorite, especially when heaped with a pretty mix of rose-tone patterns. A carved pattern in the ivory rug subtly underscores the room's floral theme.*

Right: *A pretty ruched valance and bishop's-sleeve draperies frame a patio garden just outside this spacious bedroom. A little sitting area lends the room even more versatility and appeal.* Interior designer: Cross Interiors.

Rosy Outlook

MORE WALLPAPER DESIGNS feature roses than any other motif for one simple reason: They are dependably beautiful in any style and color. The most common, best-loved roses are bright red, but their very popularity makes it challenging to use them in a fresh, creative way. One solution is to punch up the intensity with a crisp, complementary color scheme such as red, green, and white. This color combination is a favorite in decorating—the blend of warmth and brightness works well in traditional settings. In these rooms, rose-print wallpaper establishes the background, and red, white, and green prints, from gingham checks to rosy florals, carry the theme. Vintage furniture and accent pieces in red lacquer and distressed white paint complete the picture. Inspired by romantic, 18th-century English style, these rooms make the most of the power of red and the power of roses.

A chaise longue is wonderfully inviting, especially when layered with throws and pillows in a sophisticated mix of red, white, gray, and lamplight-gold. An antique red chinoiserie chest is topped with a red wire planter holding a collection of small plants. Interior designer: Susan Zises Green.

A flurry of red, white, and green prints heap this bed with exciting eye appeal. Along with the dark green easy chair, the strongly colored bed visually balances the wall of white, glass-front cabinets with their delicate, floral, shirred-fabric treatments.

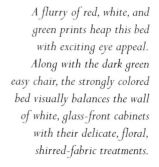

If you have the space, a complete sitting area in the bedroom makes it a versatile retreat in which you'll love to spend your time. A master suite is a great place to display fragile treasures and delicate fabrics that might not survive elsewhere in an active household.

An heirloom quilt in a host of garden-bright colors tops a goldenrod chintz bed-skirt for an old-fashioned, cozy look. The tall bed curtains are lined in the same yellow chintz to impart a golden glow.

Primary Harmony

A few grand gestures give this spacious bedroom an air that's both regal and welcoming. A four-poster bed gets the royal treatment with ceiling-height draperies in a serene floral-and-stripe print. A sitting-area sofa and simple draperies on the French doors utilize the same fabric for visual unity.
Interior designer: Joseph P. Horan.

BLUE AND GREEN ARE RELAXING, to be sure, but you must wake up as well as go to sleep in the bedroom. So if a livelier hue suits you, why not swath the space in sprightly yellow? On those rainy Monday mornings, it's an automatic mood-lifter. This spacious bedroom is all aglow and filled with cozy references to earlier times. Designed in English country style, it's hospitable and elegant. A carefully orchestrated color scheme adds rich cinnabar-red and French blue to the predominant golden hues, and the use of all three primary colors creates a serene sense of balance. Two great floral fabrics are paired with low-key prints and solids for a look that's lively but not visually cluttered. Befitting the fashion born in country houses, the elegance is tempered by a sense of ease and comfort. The result is a bedroom that is graciously inviting, day or night.

Left: *A headboard in the shape of a white picket fence is a lighthearted focal point in this bedroom. You could take a section of real fencing and create a similar effect. White wicker adds fresh charm, while an antique desk and a blue-and-white mottled chair add extra visual interest.*

Sunny Disposition

Few color schemes offer the universal appeal of cobalt blue, sunshine yellow, and white. It's attractive in a master suite, charming in a child's room, and perfect for a guest room that will be used by both sexes and various ages. If you favor a serene, uplifting look, opt for walls painted jonquil yellow, and let the interesting lines of the furniture and the strong patterns of your bedding fabrics provide the drama. If you can't get enough of a print you love, indulge in the lively look of an all-over pattern. If you choose a popular color scheme such as this trio, it should be easy to find an array of coordinates, from bedding to wallcoverings. As an alternative to using the same print, there are many groups in the same color scheme that include other prints for visual contrast.

Opposite: *This pampering bedroom takes an unusual yet charming approach to comfort via a bathtub built into a window nook. Floral wallcovering borders frame the space with gentle drama. An elaborate wrought-iron bed contributes to the romantic ambience.* Interior designer: Allison & Associates.

Pure Opulence

Chinoiserie, the Chinese (or Chinese-inspired) artistry that beguiled 18th-century Europeans and Americans, has never really gone out of style. Eastern art captures the delicate spirit of nature in a unique way that suits every style, from minimalist modern to Federalist traditional. Equally time-less and elegant are lavish draperies and screens within rooms. They're perfect for defining spaces and adding a sense of quiet luxury, but make sure the quality of art is good and the fabric yardage is generous, never skimpy. That done, a few pieces of fine furniture anchor the look. Since European and American aristocrats treasured the arts of the Orient, you can mix a "chow" table or other Asian design with almost any 18th- or 19th-century European style. Easiest of all, look for Chinese Chippendale-style furniture in reproduction today. Add an orchid or other exotic, flowering plant for the perfect accent.

A fabulous Chinese floral screen with a silvery background adds subtle glamour to a stately setting. A hand-embroidered silk pillow and throw, celadon floor vase, and wool rug evoke the 18th-century fusion of Eastern and Western artistry. Source: Gump's.

For a lavish yet elegantly subtle look, oyster damask bed curtains match those on the window overlooking the garden, and the same fabric is padded on the walls. Carefully chosen antiques and an abundance of fresh flowers add drama and color. *Interior designer: Justine Ringlien.*

Secret Gardens

Y OUR LITTLE BLOSSOM MAY grow up to be an astronaut, but let's face it, when you're decorating a young girl's room, a flower garden just naturally comes to mind. Trompe l'oeil painting is the easiest way to achieve the flexibility of continuing a scene wherever you like, as well as letting you add custom elements—a favorite puppy or swing perhaps? If your plan requires covering a relatively limited area, you may opt for stenciled designs. Laser-cut stencils allow multiple colors and wonderful detail. They're also available for large-scale effects, so you can create a flowery bower around an alcove as well as a simple garland above the bed. A quick, easy alternative is wallcovering; classic scenic papers are available, so look for those with pretty garden settings. When covered with flowers, even oddly shaped rooms lose their awkwardness and live happily ever after.

Opposite: A beautifully realized trompe l'oeil garden, complete with gazebo, birds, and birdbath, wraps this room with enchantment. The dormers and quirky angles add to the charm. An old crib makes a perfect home for Teddy and friends, while antique children's furniture is always ready for an impromptu tea party or coloring session. Above: A pretty bouquet of pink and white hydrangeas makes a garden-fresh accent underfoot. Made of pure wool with a cotton back and latex grippers for nonslip safety, this 30-inch round rug will punctuate a room with charm. Source: Gump's.

Above: Here's an easy way to find inspiration for a trompe l'oeil project: Adapt a fabric print or painting you love. The poppy-field print on the window valance reappears on the floor, with the addition of garden stepping stones. To protect a trompe l'oeil floor masterpiece, cover it with numerous coats of polyurethane. Interior designer: Norma Hayman.

Tranquil tints of rose, sage, and ivory give this old-fashioned, garden-roses bedroom eternal charm. Who wouldn't want to curl up here with a good book and a cup of tea? Using the same two prints throughout the room creates this peaceful effect, and an elaborately scrolled, garden gate-style brass bed adds outright drama.
Manufacturer: Sanderson.

Swathed in Romance

GARDEN STYLE, PERHAPS MORE than any other, has the ability to transport us to another place without our investing a lot of time and money. You don't need the best of everything to create a romantic, lighthearted living environment. These two rooms show how easy it can be to use floral prints to create a coddling personal retreat. A generous length of softly draped fabric in gentle white enhances the serene mood in one room. A pale, old-fashioned floral print, repeated on the walls and bedding, encompasses the other room in tender tints. Metal beds—a double and a single daybed—bring interestingly scrolled, airy lines to the setting in appealing contrast to plump cushions, pillows, and comforters. Add a few garden accessories, from wicker picnic baskets to pretty vases, and your retreat will soothe you through many seasons to come.

A scrolled metal daybed gains an extra dash of romance with a draped gauze canopy. Simple ticking-stripe fabric sets off the densely flowered wallpaper, floral pillows, and accessories, including a pair of celadon-painted picnic baskets. Manufacturer: Seabrook Wallcoverings.

Sweet Dreams

IF EVER A ROOM was made for the romance of garden style, it's the bedroom. When you're nestled in a bed of blossoms, even a simple catnap can feel like a midsummer night's dream. Elements that create garden-style enchantment are easy to gather, as floral motifs are more popular for the bedroom than anywhere else in the house. Start with the natural appeal of woven wicker furniture, or pick a pretty wrought-iron bed inspired by vines and leaves. The bed, storage pieces, and end tables don't need to match, so why not indulge in an armoire decorated with a trompe l'oeil garden? Add a graceful chair, a whimsical floral rug to cushion bare toes, plus a mix of floral-patterned bed linens and decorative pillows in your favorite colors. Most important, add a few fresh flowers or flowering plants to sweetly scent your intimate garden retreat.

Above: Unabashedly feminine and flirty, this pretty slipper chair with a ruffled skirt is guaranteed to give your boudoir a rosy outlook. The print of pink roses and lilacs evokes old-fashioned English country style in the best possible way.
Manufacturer: Swedish Blonde.

A classically inspired lamp base gets a casual, summerhouse feeling thanks to the weathered white finish and airy wicker shade. It's the perfect companion for wicker bedroom furniture.
Source: Coldwater Creek.

Cherry blossoms strewn across a delicate aqua background lend any bedroom the fresh look of springtime. Coordinating, silky accent pillows embroidered with cherry branches recall intricate Asian artistry. To avoid monotony and tie in the wall color, add a few white or solid-color pillowcases. Source: Coldwater Creek.

Diminutive charmers like this little pot of African violets make a garden nook of an ordinary end table, nightstand, or book-shelf. Pick species that thrive in the amount of light each location provides, or use faux plants anywhere. For an accent, large, flat leaves tied with raffia or ribbon make charming covers around florist pots.
Manufacturer: NDI.

An iron bed recalls vintage garden gates and fences, so you need only to toss on floral bedding for instant garden ambience. This charming reproduction of an antique French daybed is available in two antiqued finishes, rust or French green. Source: Ballard Designs.

This limited-edition, scenic armoire is a spectacular focal point as well as a practical storage solution. The masterful trompe l'oeil painting gives the illusion of depth and celebrates the glories of a rustic garden. Manufacturer: Habersham. Source: Porters of Racine.

Comfort underfoot can be an eye-catching decorative element. This lovely, pure wool rug, worked in soft tints, delivers garden style as fresh as spring. In a bedroom that gets little foot traffic, why not indulge in pale hues and give your color scheme a lighthearted look? Manufacturer: Asmara, Inc.

Resource Directory

Architects

Quinn Evans Architects
1214 28th Street NW
Washington, DC 20007
phone 202-298-6700
fax 202-298-6666
contact-us@quinnevans.com
www.quinnevans.com
(91)

Builders

Alpine Log Homes, Inc.
2666 Hwy. 93 North
Victor, MT 59875
phone 406-642-3451
www.alpineloghomes.com
(14)

Interior Designers

Accent On Design
2005 De La Cruz Boulevard
#145
Santa Clara, CA 95050
phone 408-988-4600
(8, 80)

Allison & Associates
2154 Chestnut Avenue
Buena Vista, VA 24416
phone 540-261-1723
(117)

Sande Chernett Interiors
2 Haver Hill Court
Beachwood, OH 44122
phone 216-591-9400
(49)

The Comfort Common
717 High Street
Comfort, TX 78013
phone 830-995-3030
fax 830-995-3455
comfortcommon@hctc.net
www.comfortcommon.com
(22)

Country Floors
15 East 16th Street
New York, NY 10003
phone 212-627-8300
(96)

Madison Cox
220 W. 19th Street
New York, NY 10002
phone 212-242-4631
(24, 30)

Gary Crain
215 East 58th Street
New York, NY 10022
phone 212-223-2050
(68)

Cross Interiors
Cheryl Casey Ross
6712 Colbath Avenue
Van Nuys, CA 91405
phone 818-988-2047
cherylcaseyross@cross
    interiors.com
www.crossinteriors.com
(8, 110–111)

Design 1/Marilee Schemp
The Summit Opera House
497 Springfield Avenue
Summit, NJ 07901
phone 908-277-1110
(64)

**D'Image/Fran Murphy
    & Associates**
71 E. Allendale Road
Saddle River, NJ 07458
phone 201-934-5420
(40)

Susan Zises Green
11 East 44th Street
New York, NY 10017
phone 212-867-2980
(112)

The Hammer & Nail
232 Madison Avenue
Wyckoff, NJ 07481
phone 201-891-5252
fax 201-891-0751
info@thehammerandnail.com
www.thehammerandnail.com
(41)

Norma Hayman
5 Hartshorne Lane
Rumson, NJ 07760
phone 732-219-0137
(120)

Joseph Horan
3299 Washington Street
San Francisco, CA 94115
phone 415-346-5646
fax 415-922-0719
hor347@aol.com
www.designfinder.com/horan
(46, 47, 104–105, 114–115)

Melinda Kuehne
Heart of America
370 W. Bridge Street
New Hope, PA 18938
phone 215-862-3304
fax 215-862-2931
(90)

Stacey Lapuk
437 Wellesley Avenue
Mill Valley, CA 94941
phone 415-383-9223
(60, 61)

**Barbara Ostrom
    & Associates**
One International Boulevard
Suite 209
Mahwah, NJ 07495
phone 201-529-0444
(62–63, 73)

Durene Phillipo Designs
5215 Capital Boulevard
Raleigh, NC 27616
phone 919-8873-1666
(37)

Ann Platz & Co.
1266 W. Paces Ferry Road
Suite 521
Atlanta, GA 30327
phone 404-237-1000
fax 404-237-3810
annplatz@flash.net
www.annplatz.com
(6)

Razvi Design Studio
14829 Penasquitos Court
San Diego, CA 92129
phone/fax 858-672-8831
Arazvi@san.rr.com
(85)

Justine Ringlien
96 Ridgeview Drive
Atherton, CA 94027
phone 650-233-0330
fax 650-854-7733
(27, 119)

Manufacturers

Artistic Tile & Stone
824 Bransten Road
San Carlos, CA 94070
phone 877-ART-TILE
info@877arttile.com
www.artistictile.net
(56)

Asmara, Inc.
88 Black Falcon Avenue
Suite 188
Boston, MA 02210
phone 800-451-7240
fax: 617-261-0228
info@asmarainc.com
www.asmarainc.com
(79, 125)

Avanti Linens
234 Moonachie Road
Moonachie, NJ 07074
phone 201-641-7766
fax 201-641-1712
info@avantilinens.com
www.avantilinens.com
(100)

**Brewster Wallcovering
    Company**
67 Pacella Park Drive
Randolph, MA 02368
phone 800-366-1700
fax 781-963-4885
www.brewsterwallcovering.com
(94–95)

Habersham
P.O. Box 1209
Toccoa, GA 30577
phone 800-HABERSHAM
(125)

Jacuzzi Whirlpool Bath
2121 N. California Boulevard
Suite 475
Walnut Creek, CA 94596
phone 925-938-7070
fax 925-938-3025
www.jacuzzi.com
(81)

Kohler
444 Highland Drive
Kohler, WI 53044
phone 800-456-4537
www.kohler.com
(89, 100)

Maine Cottage Furniture
P.O. Box 935
Yarmouth, ME 04096
phone 207-846-1430
fax 207-846-0602
info@mainecottage.com
www.mainecottage.com
(9, 15)

Michaelian & Kohlberg
121 East 5th Avenue
Hendersonville, NC 28792
phone 828-697-1574
fax 828-697-9084
design@mkhome.com
www.mkhome.com
(33, 79)

Natural Decorations, Inc. (NDI)
P.O. Box 847
Brewton, AL 36427
phone 800-522-2627
fax 877-578-5101
ndi@ndi.com
www.ndi.com
(22, 28, 33, 37, 52, 56, 62, 66, 70, 108, 124)

PierceMartin
Chip Cheatham, designer
99 Armour Drive
Atlanta, GA 30324
phone 800-334-8701
(79)

Renaissance Conservatories
132 Ashmore Drive
Leola, PA 17540
phone 800-882-4657
fax 717-661-7727
www.renaissance-online.com
(12, 26)

Sanderson
Sanderson House
Oxford Road, Denham
UB9 4DX, UK
phone 011-44-1895-830-044
fax 011-44-1895-830-055
cvc@a-sanderson.co.uk
www.sanderson-online.co.uk
(57, 122)

Seabrook Wallcoverings
1325 Farmville Road
Memphis, TN 38122
phone 800-238-9152
fax 901-320-3673
www.seabrookwallcoverings.com
(7, 16, 17, 19, 39, 45, 48, 51, 88, 109, 123)

Stroheim & Romann
31–11 Thomson Avenue
Long Island City, NY 11101
phone 718-706-7000
(7, 52, 72, 108)

Summer Classics
#1 Summer Classics Way
Columbiana, AL 35051
phone 205-669-9977
fax 205-669-2571
sclassics@aol.com
www.summerclassics.com
(33, 78, 101)

Swedish Blonde
P.O. Box 617
Madison, NC 27025
phone 800-274-9096
fax 336-548-6225
www.swedish-blonde.com
(102, 124, 127)

Walker Zanger
8901 Bradley Avenue
Sun Valley, CA 91352
phone 310-798-6919
fax 310-798-6909
www.walkerzanger.com
(57)

Waverly
Div. of FSC Wallcoverings
79 Madison Avenue
New York, NY 10016
phone 212-213-7900
fax 212-213-7640
www.fschumacher.com
(53)

Photographers

Abode UK
Albion Court
1 Pierce Street
Macclesfield, Cheshire
SK11 6ER ENGLAND
phone 011-44-1625-500-070
fax 011-44-1625-500-910
(10, 28, 31, 42, 43, 58, 69, 74–75)

Dennis Anderson
680 Point San Pedro Road
San Rafael, CA 94901
phone 415-457-1998
fax 415-457-3922
dennis@dandersonphoto.com
www.dandersonphoto.com
(27, 119)

Bill Bolin
1176 Mississippi Avenue
Dallas, TX 75207
phone 214-631-4848
(56)

Jim Brady
1010 University Avenue
#823
San Diego, CA 92103
phone/fax 619-296-5304
(85)

Mark Bryant
817 S. Higgins

Missoula, MT 59801
phone 406-721-2414
(14)

Jane Davis
P.O. Box 6534
Annapolis, MD 21401
phone 410-841-6739
fax 410-849-2015
(32)

Michael Duncan
4400 Bayou Boulevard
Suite 32B
Pensacola, FL 32503
phone 850-476-5035
fax 850-476-1556
michael@duncanmccall.com
www.duncanmccall.com
(22, 28, 33, 37, 52, 56, 62, 66, 70, 108, 124)

Phillip Ennis
114 Millertown Road
Bedford, NY 10506
phone 516-379-4273
fax 516-379-1126
(18, 24, 29, 30, 38, 40, 62–64, 66–68, 70–71, 73, 76, 83, 96, 98–99, 112–113)

Nancy Hill
210 Mamanasco Road
Ridgefield, CA 06877
phone 203-431-7655
(13, 20, 34, 36, 55, 82, 97)

The Interior Archive, Ltd.
6 Colville Mews
Lonsdale Road
London W11 2DA, UK
phone 011-44-020-7221-9922
(77)

Jim Koch Studio, Inc.
109 W. Southpoint Avenue
High Point, NC 27260
phone 336-887-6677
(125)

Mark Lohman
1021 S. Fairfax Avenue
Los Angeles, CA 90019
phone 323-933-3359
fax 310-471-6268
(5, 21, 23, 44, 86–87, 92–93, 106)

Melabee M. Miller
29 Beechwood Place
Hillside, NJ 07205
phone 908-527-9121
fax 908-527-0242
(90, 120)

Samu Studios
P.O. Box 165
Bay Port, NY 11705
phone 212-754-0415
www.samustudios.com
(107)

Brad Simmons
870 Craintown Road
Perryville, KY 40468
phone 859-332-8400
fax 859-332-4433
(22, 37, 50, 84, 116–117)

Tim Street-Porter
2074 Watsonia Terrace
Hollywood, CA 90068
phone 323-874-4278
(25, 54, 65, 121)

John Sutton
8 Main Street
Point San Quentin, CA 94964
phone 415-258-8100
fax 415-258-8167
john@johnsutton.com
www.johnsutton.com
(60, 61)

Brian Vanden Brink
39 Curtis Avenue
Camden, ME 04843
phone 207-236-4035
(91)

Retailers

Ballard Designs
1670 Defoor Avenue
Atlanta, GA 30318
phone 800-367-2775
www.ballarddesigns.com
(32, 35, 44, 50, 56, 79, 100–101, 125, 127)

Brennan-Edwards, Inc.
196 Prince George Street
Annapolis, MD 21401
phone 410-267-9437
(32)

Coldwater Creek
One Coldwater Creek Drive
Sandpoint, ID 83864
phone 800-968-0984
www.coldwatercreek.com
(33, 72, 100, 124, 126)

Gump's
135 Post Street
San Francisco, CA 94108
phone 800-882-8055
www.gumps.com
(33, 101, 118, 120, 126)

Krupps
2011 Sheridan Avenue
Lennon, MI 48449
phone 888-578-7771
fax 810-621-4577
www.kruppsdecor.com
(32)

Porters of Racine
301 6th Street
Racine, WI 53403
phone 800-558-3245
fax 262-633-5011
porterad@wi.net
www.portersofracine.com
(125)

Quoizel
590 Old Willets Path
Hauppauge, NY 11788
phone 631-273-2700
fax 631-231-7102
www.quoizelonline.com
(57)

Smith & Hawken
Corporate Offices
4 Hamilton Landing
Novato, CA 94949
phone 800-776-3336
www.smithandhawken.com
(32, 78, 126)

Spiegel Catalog, Inc.
3500 Lacey Road
Downers Grove, IL 60515
phone 800-345-4500
fax 630-769-3686
www.spiegel.com
(57, 78)

Wisteria
P.O. Box 7877
Dallas, TX 75209
phone 800-320-9757
fax 214-969-7311
customerservice@wisteria.com
www.wisteria.com
(56)

Photo Credits

Front cover: **Jamie Hadley Photographer**

Back cover: **Joseph P. Horan, FASID/John Vaughan**

Abode UK: 10, 28 (left), 31, 42, 43, 58, 69, 74, 75; **Accent on Design/Quadra Focus:** 8 (bottom), 80; **Alpine Log Homes, Inc./Mark Bryant:** 14; **Artistic Tile, Inc./Richard Speedy:** 56 (bottom left); **Asmara, Inc./Jim Koch Studio, Inc.:** endsheets, 79 (top left), 125 (bottom right); **Avanti Linens:** 100 (bottom left); **Ballard Designs:** contents; 32 (bottom center) 35, 44 (right), 50 (right), 56 (bottom right), 79 (bottom left), 100 (top right), 101 (top left & top right), 125 (top right), 127; **Brennan-Edwards, Inc./Jane Davis Photography:** 32 (top); **Brewster Wallcovering:** 94, 95; **Sande Chernett Interior Design:** 49; **Coldwater Creek, Inc.:** contents, 33 (top right), 72 (right), 100 (bottom right), 124 (center & bottom left), 126 (bottom); **Cross Interiors/Leonard Lammi Photography:** 8 (top), 110, 111; **Phillip H. Ennis Photography:** 18, 24, 29, 30, 38, 40, 62 (left), 63, 64, 66 (left), 67, 68, 70 (left), 71, 73, 76, 83, 96, 98, 99, 112, 113; **Gump's:** contents, 33 (bottom center), 101 (bottom left), 118, 120 (right), 126 (center); **The Hammer & Nail:** 41; **Habersham/Porters of Racine:** 125 (left); **Nancy Hill:** 20, 34; Jan Burket Interior Design: 55; Cernan Builders: 97; Interior by Stephanie Strokes, Inc.: 13; Kitchen Design Studio: 36; Gayle Monahan: 82; **Joseph P. Horan, FASID/John Vaughan:** 46, 47, 104, 105, 114, 115; **The Interior Archive, Ltd./Fritz von der Schulenburg:** 77; **Jacuzzi Whirlpool Bath:** 81; **Kohler Co.:** 89, 100 (top left); **Krupps.com/Rome Industries:** contents, 32 (bottom left); **Stacey Lapuk Interior Design, Inc./John Sutton:** contents, 60, 61; **Maine Cottage Furniture:** 9, 15; **Mark Lohman Photography:** 5, 21, 23, 44 (left), 86, 87, 92, 93, 106; **Melabee M. Miller Photography:** 90, 120 (left); **Michaelian & Kohlberg:** 33 (bottom left), 79 (top right); **Natural Decorations, Inc.:** contents, 22 (left), 28 (right), 33 (top left), 37 (right), 52 (right), 56 (top left), 62 (right), 66 (right), 70 (right), 108 (right), 124 (bottom right); **PierceMartin:** 79 (bottom); **Ann Platz/PRO Studio:** 6; **Quoizel:** 57 (bottom left); **Razvi Design Studio/Jim Brady Photography:** 85; **Renaissance Conservatories:** contents, 12, 26; **Justine Ringlien/dandersonphoto.com:** contents, 27, 119; **Samu Studios:** 107; **Sanderson:** 57 (bottom center), 122; **Brad Simmons Photography:** 22 (right), 37 (left), 50 (left), 84, 116, 117; **Smith & Hawken:** 32 (right center), 78 (top left), 126 (left); **Spiegel Catalog, Inc.:** 57 (top right), 78 (top right); Jeff McNamara: 57 (top left); **Tim Street-Porter Photography:** 25, 121; Barbara Barry: 65; Bob & Isabel Higgins, Designers: 54; **Stroheim & Romann:** 7 (right), 52 (left), 72 (left), 108 (left); **Summer Classics:** 33 (bottom right), 78 (bottom), 101 (center); **Swedish Blonde Corporation/Stephanie von Ohain:** 102, 124 (top), 127 (bottom); **Thompson & Co./Seabrook Wallcoverings:** 88; "Above & Beyond" 16; "Cheri Blum", Sandpiper Studios 19; "Cuttin' Up" 39, 48; "Little Garden Handbook" 7 (left), 109; "Judy Buswell Watercolors" 17, 45, 51, 123; **Brian Vanden Brink:** 91; **Walker Zanger:** 57 (bottom right); **Waverly, a division of FSC Wallcoverings:** 53; **Wisteria:** 56 (top right).